The Blood Covenant

Pastor Olusegun Raji

The Blood Covenant

Copyright © 2020 by Pastor Olusegun Raji

All rights reserved. No part of this book may be reproduced or transmitted in any form or by any means without the written permission of the author.

Good News Translation® (Today's English Version, Second Edition) Copyright © 1992 American Bible Society. All rights reserved.

Scripture taken from the New King James Version ®. Copyright © 1982 by Thomas Nelson, Inc. Used by permission.

All rights reserved.

Published by:
Eleviv Publishing Group
www.elevivpublishing.com
info@elevivpublishing.com
1-800-353-0635
1-281-857-0569

ISBN: 978-1-952744-13-6

Printed in the United States of America

10 9 8 7 6 5 4 3 2

DEDICATION

This book is specially dedicated to the Almighty God, the Creator of the universe, who sent His only begotten son Jesus Christ to save my soul and qualify me to be one of the partakers of the divine nature in Christ Jesus.

ACKNOWLEDGMENTS

I would like to express my special gratitude to the Almighty God for the inspiration to write this book. From the depths of my heart, I love and appreciate my wife, Pastor Omolegho Raji, for her love, encouragement, and unique support in prayer.

I am also grateful for my five wonderful children (Iyanuoluwa, Iyinoluwa, Inioluwa, Ireoluwa, and Ibukunoluwa); for their love, unending supports, and prayers to complete the scripts. Thank you all for proofreading the script and making this dream a reality.

I would also like to thank my spiritual children worldwide, especially at RCCG Chapelle De La Resurrection Gatineau, Quebec.

Thanks to my publishing team and the book cover designer.

I appreciate you all. May the Lord bless you always in Jesus name! Amen!

FOREWORD

As believers, sometimes, we lose faith in ourselves and in life for different reasons, and it's okay because we are humans, therefore, imperfect. As believers, we must always remember that embracing the Word of God and believing in the strength of His blood, the blood, will heal us from pain and brokenness, uplift us from doubts, hopelessness, and emptiness, guard us from sins and evil doers, and guide us on the right path.

Let us also remember that salvation comes by believing. It comes with a strong belief in the death and resurrection of Jesus Christ on the cross. This book is all about showing us how to access the blessings of the covenant through faith in the Lord Jesus. This beautifully written expose on 'Blood Covenant' and the efficacy of the power in 'the blood of Jesus' will expose the strength and the weakness of our faith to us. God's love for us earns us the gift of salvation. The blood truly speaks for us, heals us, cleanses us of our iniquities, and gives us the assurance of eternity. The blood of Jesus that was shed on the cross cleanses your sins and mine, and it also purifies us.

I love the personal stories, accounts, and experiences in this book. I strongly believe they will help drive home the message.

Vivian Okojie

TABLE OF CONTENTS

WHAT A COVENANT IS 1

UNDERSTANDING THE BLOOD COVENANT 9

CONNECTING TO THE COVENANT 15

THE GENERATIONAL CONSEQUENCES OF A COVENANT 27

ACCESSING THE BLESSINGS OF COVENANTS 33

THE COVENANT OF MULTIPLICATION 41

THE COVENANT OF PROSPERITY 49

THE COVENANT OF FRUITFULNESS 59

KNOWING YOUR IDENTITY IN CHRIST 65

LIVING BY FAITH 73

TOTAL OBEDIENCE 81

LOVE FOR GOD AND MAN 87

THE ROLE OF PRAYERS 95

GENEROUS GIVING 101

BALANCING YOUR FAITH WITH WORKS 109

EPILOGUE 115

WHAT A COVENANT IS

Years ago, a rich man gathered his two sons to his bedside for a heart-to-heart chat. They were grown men with families of their own. He was satisfied with how their lives had turned out. Having lost his wife, their mother, a few years after the birth of his youngest son, he could not have been more grateful.

While talking to them, he reminded them of the principles he'd taught them, charging them to be of one mind, united in thoughts and intentions. They were to continue managing his estate, which included a flourishing business chain, two NGOs catering to orphans and widows, investments in real estate, agriculture, and mortgages. They would find directions on projects they were to execute, he said, in a will prepared by his lawyers. There were clearly stated instructions the sons were to follow, traditions he desired that they observed, and several other caveats.

Before all that, there were conditions the two sons were to fulfill to lay claim to the portions disbursed to them. His voice lowering, he signaled for the first son to lean in and whispered into his ear. Then he repeated the same for the younger son. He asked if they agreed to do what he'd requested of them, and they both replied in the affirmative. Satisfied, he smiled at them, drew his last breath, and was gone.

The boys set out to meet the conditions attached to their respective portions. The father had told them they only had a window of six months. A little while later, they learned that the will had not been shared in equal halves. The realization threw them into contention. The one who had gotten a more significant portion believed he was more deserving of it and the son with a lesser bit believed he deserved more. They became so embittered with each other that they parted ways, each desperate to tick off all requirements within the stipulated time.

As time wore on, the distance between the sons grew, yet the conditions remained unmet. With only a few days left, they agreed to a resolution. But it was too late. They would not meet the requirements, and eventually, they could not become partakers of the inheritance.

What a Covenant Is

As I compiled this book, my greatest desire was to help you understand the blessings you have because you believe. Something has been written for every child of God, sealed by different covenants established in the Bible. Many believers struggle to access the fullness of all we have in God because we lack thorough knowledge of the principles and covenants guiding God's blessings.

I ask you today to give full attention to know what the Word of God says about you. As a child of God, it is not about what people say, but what the Word says. How much of what the Bible says about you have you understood? God would want His children to possess that which is rightly theirs in Christ, but how do you possess that which you do not know you have?

So, what is a covenant? The Dictionary defines a covenant as an agreement, usually formal, between two or more persons, to do or not to do something specific. A covenant is different from a contract. If you have a contract, you have a deal with equal people. If one of them does not fulfill the conditions of the contract, you can break the contract. A covenant is different. A covenant is something that is written as an agreement, sealed by an individual. A covenant can also be compared to a testament, bound by conditions that are often made known to all participating parties. Before you can partake of the blessings contained in a covenant, you will be made aware of the condition(s) of the covenant. When you fulfill the condition(s) of this covenant, you can come and receive the blessings.

We often see parents engage the system of a covenant in financial dealings with their children. Parents, perhaps dissatisfied with the young ones' attitudes towards money, would set up a trust fund and include conditions like, "Until you graduate from college, you don't have access to the fund." So, the money is rightfully theirs, but they cannot access it if the attached condition wasn't met.

There are situations where one of the parties involved isn't too pleased with the entire arrangement, but as long as it is a covenant and the conditions are met, the terms remain valid. That is how covenants are wired.

Since the beginning of time, God has operated and dealt with men through the systems of covenants. Before Abraham, God had spoken to the forefathers, had committed instructions into their hands, and even asked them questions. In the third chapter of Genesis, He asks the man, Adam, how he knew he was naked. Certainly, God knew how Adam came to be naked, but because He desired to hear what the man would say for a response, God asked him.

What a Covenant is

As we have noted, covenants involve a mutual agreement between the two parties. It cannot be forced on a person, nor can it be imposed upon an individual. God's nature allows us to choose whether we would do what He asks, or not. From the Old Testament down to the New Testament, which we live in, God gives man the ability to choose.

This same option of choice applies to anyone who would come into the Kingdom of Christ. *"If you confess that Jesus is Lord and believe that God raised him from death, you will be saved" (Romans 10:9, GNT)*. Do you see that? The invitation into Christendom is structured as a covenant too. God guarantees salvation to everyone who would receive it, but the condition is that you must believe in your heart and confess with your mouth. Those are the conditions, and irrespective of time or place or location or opinion, they do not change; they cannot change.

Many people struggle to accept the gospel because they think it is too easy or too good to be true. You mean all I have to do is believe that Jesus died, and God raised Him from the dead, and confess Him as Lord? That's it? No, it's not possible. There has to be more. The truth is there isn't anymore. When a covenant is set in motion, it is set in motion. Its conditions do not change with time.

I once knew a man who made a promise to his son and daughter. "If you devote time to your academics, ranking in the top percentile at the end of each academic session, I will surprise you with gifts." The condition was this: 'finish in the top percentile,' and the reward was this: 'surprise gift per individual, per academic session.'

The Blood Covenant

So, if the man decided that, for a surprise, he would take his kids to see a movie, they couldn't complain because the type of gift was not specified. If he decided to buy his son a skateboard and his daughter a 24-karat gold wristwatch, they would receive the gifts with gladness of heart. Why? The man did not define what his surprises would be. Once his kids agreed to it, they also agreed to the spontaneity of the surprise.

Likewise, God's covenants with us in His word. God started with Abraham. In Genesis 12, the Bible records:

The LORD said to Abram, *"Leave your country, your relatives, and your father's home, and go to a land that I am going to show you. I will give you many descendants, and they will become a great nation. I will bless you and make your name famous so that you will be a blessing. I will bless those who bless you, but I will curse those who curse you. And through you, I will bless all the nations." (verses 1-3)* GNT

We see here the call to Abraham (God had not yet rewritten his name). God was setting in motion a script that would play out over generations to come, but first, He needed to begin with Abraham. God says, "Abraham, I need you to leave this place where you are familiar with everything. I need you to take this walk of faith and leave, leave the solitude of your father's house and embark on a journey that I will lead you through. It is a journey of faith."

Why Abraham? We may not know from scriptures why God chose Abraham and not someone else, but we understand why Abraham had to go out on a limb. God was instituting something that would extend beyond man, beyond the Son, which God would give him, beyond his grandchildren. God was prepared to make a generational covenant with Abraham, but the foundation had to be laid right. It had to be built on faith.

So, Abraham ups and leaves his father's house, taking with him Sarah (God had not yet rewritten her name) and Lot, his cousin. As they journey, we find records of their encounters with Pharaoh, king of Egypt, the war at the Valley of Siddim, Abraham's conquest, and his encounter with Melchizedek, king of Salem, a divinely arranged meeting.

Then we arrive at the fifteenth chapter of Genesis, where God presents Abraham with another covenant.

"Then and there the Lord made a covenant with Abram. He said, 'I promise to give your descendants all this land from the border of Egypt to the Euphrates River." (Genesis 15:18) NKJV

At this time, there was no Isaac, no Ishmael, no family. God establishes a covenant with Abraham and with his seed. We might wonder and become confused, knowing that Abraham had no offspring born of him. The blessing was to Abraham and his seed to the end that we all may become partakers of it, even in this new dispensation. We sing "Abraham blessings are mine; Abraham blessings are mine," because God created a clause that allowed us to become covenant makers like Abraham through faith.

But there was a condition that was spelled out for this covenant to be fulfilled, the covenant that He had with Abraham. When we turn to the seventeenth chapter, we see the conditions earmarked for Abraham:

The Blood Covenant

When Abram was ninety-nine years old, the Lord appeared to Abram and said unto him, *"I am the Almighty God. Obey me and always do what is right. I will make my covenant with you and give you many descendants." (17:1-2)*

God essentially said to Abraham, "Remember my words which I spoke to you a while back? I am set to fulfill them, even unto your generations yet to come. All I ask is that you walk before me, as I would ask you to do."

What is crucial to note about these encounters is that, with covenants, God doesn't give us instructions or conditions to fulfill! Instead, He commits instructions to us. In the place of running with words from God, God is with us – He is not the enemy, He is not the foe, He is our help.

When we reflect on several experiences of people of faith, of Gideon, of Jephthah, of Miriam, of Deborah, and many more, we see that God was willing to help them do what He'd asked them to do, so He could do what He wanted to do for and in them. How often do we miss out on something God asked us to do, a seed He instructed us to give, a prayer session we skipped because we were tired, a time we should have said something pleasant to someone but didn't, and then we think God is suddenly our enemy, happy that we didn't do what He would have us do?

God delights when we align with His thoughts, His leadings. We are called to do His will, but He's more interested in us doing His will than we ever can bring ourselves to be. He was willing to help Abraham's faith for as long as Abraham needed it, to the end that He may fulfill His covenant with Abraham.

What a Covenant is

If a friend introduces you to a profitable business and asks that you invest alongside her but then goes out of her way to help you get the funds you need to join them. Eventually, she hands you your equal share of the profits. That's God, but He does so much more.

The Apostle Paul captures a facet of God's benevolence in saying, *"But God has shown us how much He loves us – it was while we were still sinners that Christ died for us." (Romans 5:8, NKJV)* Isn't that such a great joy – to know God is heavily invested in our following His will, that He may bless us accordingly? To this end, we must understand how we are made righteous in Christ. What did Christ give us on the cross? Christ came to establish a new covenant. How did He do this? What is the significance of the shedding of the blood on the cross? Our comprehension of this reality would enable us to lay hold of all we have received in Christ.

UNDERSTANDING THE BLOOD COVENANT

The renowned 19th-century American preacher Robert Lowry is credited with over five hundred hymn melodies, writing music to remarkable hymns like "I Need Thee Every Hour" and "All the Way My Savior Leads Me." In 1876, Lowry composed the heart-rendering piece, "Nothing but The Blood of Jesus," an expression of his heart and character.

The lyrics, which are still sung in the church today, pay cognizance to the power in the shed blood of Jesus Christ. Consider the chorus which reads thus: Oh, precious is the flow / that makes me white as snow / no other fount I know / nothing but the blood of Jesus. Lowry's life and ministry as a hymn writer epitomized his convictions in the provisions we have as believers, the blood being one of these.

In the account, according to Prophet Isaiah, the Lord appeals to His people, *"You are stained red with sin, but I will wash you as clean as snow..." (Isaiah 1:18, GNT).* By this, the Lord alludes to the coming of Christ in the flesh and His sacrifice on the cross. The blood of Jesus Christ administrates a cleansing and renewal for everyone who comes to God through Jesus Christ.

When we begin to reflect on the blood covenant, we can walk back into the Saints' experiences. Knowing that every covenant contained in scriptures included two parties, we should ask ourselves: What were the conditions surrounding the Old Testament's covenant? What does the New Testament covenant – through the blood of Jesus – entail?

The Blood of the New Covenant

"In the same way, after the supper, he took the cup and said, 'This cup is God's new covenant, sealed with my blood. Whenever you drink it, do so in memory of me. This means that every time you eat this bread and drink from this cup, you proclaim the Lord's death until He comes." (1 Corinthians 11:25-26). In these scriptures, the apostle Paul offers us a recapping of the experience of the Last Supper. The Last Supper represents Jesus's invitation to us to become partakers of the new covenant which He brings to us from the Father, the covenant of life eternal. It stands as the basis for our participation in the Holy Communion, during which we eat the bread and drink the wine as symbols of the body and the blood of Christ.

The blood is an essential component of living. There is an average of five liters of blood in an adult body, varying based on age and size. The blood accounts for approximately 8% of the adult's body weight and about 10% of an infant's body weight. The blood is the life-giving element of any human. Thus, a covenant predicated on the blood is very potent. As the Israelites journeyed towards the promised land, God handed them several commandments on living, some of those relating to what they ate and how they ate them. God said, *"Only do not eat meat with blood still in it, for the life is in the blood, and you must not eat the life with the meat." (Deuteronomy 12:23)* The consequence of obeying this instruction was a blessing not only to the Israelites but to their children to come.

The Blood Covenant

It was 2020, and we hardly needed to be warned to desist from eating blood. With the new trends are creeping upon us and the advancement in technology, I couldn't imagine what would happen to a person who decided to eat blood. Maybe they'd go viral and get lots of backlashes online. However, it's more important that we give much diligence to knowing the reason for the new covenant we have in God, sealed by the blood of Jesus Christ. Not because of any strange tradition or rules about blood but because of who Jesus is.

When Jesus went to the Cross, the blood that gushed out of him is the life of God that was put on the altar so we can have free access to God. Remember that under the old covenant's operational system, the high priest must make sacrifices for sin.

There was the sin offering, the grain offering, and the yearly offering the priest made both for himself and the people. God introduced the people to a medium of exchange – where the people could transfer their volume of iniquities to the chosen animal, a lamb or a goat, and in exchange be declared sin-free, innocent, for the period which the sacrifice was valid.

We can liken it to a subscription to a data plan or a monthly Netflix plan. Suppose you subscribed for three months, and for those ninety days, you have the freedom to roam the app, download, and watch as many movies as you want. You could decide to ignore your work, forget your family, and just watch. Not a good idea, but people do so.

The moment your subscription expires, access is denied. You have no access to the app, to the movies. Of course, the app remains on your smartphone device, but except you chose an auto-renewal service, you couldn't do anything on the app. You can whine and murmur all day, but until you pay that money, you can't do anything.

This was how the Israelites operated. Once the atonement expired, they had to do another one. The book of Leviticus contains several of such sacrifices, of the slaying of lambs and sheep. Yet, it never really was enough until Christ.

On the cross, Jesus did an entire substitution. He introduced a new operational system, where the only requirement for functionality and access was His blood. The book of Hebrews tells us that Jesus Christ *"does not need to offer sacrifices every day for his sins first and then for the sins of the people. He offered one sacrifice, once and for all when He offered Himself." (7:27).*

Jesus paid it all, and He paid it once and for all, with His blood. The blood of Jesus carries the life of Jesus, and as He bled on the cross, He established an exchange – His life for ours. Sometimes, we joke, "Jesus died for man's sins already, and I don't need to die again." And that is the truth. His blood, the blood of the only begotten Son, is always more than sufficient to seal us in the New Covenant.

Let's go back to our Netflix Example. Now suppose that instead of a subscription, you somehow become friends with a stakeholder at Netflix. Or that you somehow become the principal front-end developer or the Head of Operations at Netflix Inc. Would you still need to do a monthly subscription? Or rather, isn't a monthly subscription only required for someone who creates an account? We can assume that your access to the app would be all-time access.

Jesus has given us all-time access to the Father. By virtue of His death, He rent the veil which separated us from the Father. Now we can come boldly, without having to offer a lamb for atonement. This access we have, this covenant, is sealed by the blood of Jesus.

What else does the blood of Jesus do?

The blood links us to a new adoption. In Africa, we are often exposed to the nature of a blood covenant. There are several experiences of people who had blood covenants done on their behalf. A father would head to a coven to enact a covenant because he desires to protect his children and believes the coven is the right call. You would find that these covenants often necessitate the offering of an innocent life; a life for another life.

On becoming Christians, people who have a prior covenant hanging over them are now established in the new operation secured by the blood of Jesus Christ. Anyone who believes has the life-giving blood of Jesus Christ running through him, and so a new covenant replaces that of old. For as many as receive Him, to them, God gives the power to become sons (John 1:12), and in them, the blood of Jesus Christ flows. There's an adoption, an induction into sonship, facilitated by Christ's blood.

We have confidence before the Father. You can go into the presence of the Father. Hallelujah! Yes, this is the confidence we have in approaching Him. *"We have, then, my friends, complete freedom to go into the Most Holy Place by means of the death of Jesus. He opened for us a new way, a living way, through the curtain – that is, through His own body. We have a great priest in charge of the house of God. So, let us come near to God with a sincere heart and a sure faith, with hearts that have been purified from a guilty conscience and with bodies washed with clean water." (Hebrews 10:19 – 22)*

Understanding the Blood Covenant

The commandment here for us is that we should draw near to Him with full assurance of faith. But what is the full assurance of faith? It's that when we come to God, we have the confidence that He hears us. He hears us, yes. And we have this confidence, yes. But how can we have this confidence? It says, "Our heart should be sprinkled from an evil conscience our body wash as with pure water." So, the blood of Jesus cleanses us, rids us of a guilt-ridden conscience. Hallelujah!

The blood cleanses us. We see from Isaiah that the blood has cleansing power. It makes us as white as snow. This whitening, this cleansing, as though with the purest of waters, is not a physical one. It takes place within the heart. How do you know a man is saved? Once he believes and confesses the Lord Jesus, a man is saved. Does his hair grow longer? Does he become funnier or taller? Of course not.

Similarly, the cleansing of our hearts isn't evidenced by a wrinkle-free face or glowing skin. It is within us – in our souls and our spirits. It is also eternal. We are rid of all guilt, all wrongdoing, all pricked conscience, through the blood of Jesus.

God is our Judge. We stand before Him, Who searches the innermost parts of man. I tell you, it is not about what people; it is about what the Word of God says. What does the Word of God say about you and your conscience? This is why we keep admonishing believers not to stay away from the bible. Our identity, our realities, our expectations, and experiences are all contained in the Word of God.

The more time you spend fellowshipping with God through Christ by the Holy Spirit, the more you are transformed into the fullness of all God has prepared for you, sealed by the precious blood of Jesus Christ.

Connecting to the Covenant

If you had to join a virtual meeting on your laptop, you'd want it fully charged. Imagine a meeting scheduled to last three hours and where you have to take notes and listen closely to what each speaker shares. You wouldn't want to miss anything. Halfway through, you glance at the lower end of the screen and notice the battery life has halved.

This wouldn't have been surprising if an interrupted supply of electricity were an everyday occurrence in the country. However, you are not in such a place, the electricity supply is good, and there's no power outage. Yet you notice that on hovering your mouse over, the battery indicator was at 53%.

The charger is plugged into the socket and looks functional. You are naturally concerned. You switch off the socket and then, on, thinking perhaps, you haven't connected it well. Nothing changes. You repeat the motion, off and on, but nothing. You mute yourself and tap the laptop's battery. Still no change.

At this point, you are beginning to panic. You shift your seat backwards, and as you stand, your leg hits the charger's wire. At that moment, the wire falls off the table. All the while, you have thought the charger was broken, or something was wrong with the PC. Meanwhile, the issue wasn't a damaged adaptor, but the charging pin that didn't fit into the charging port in the PC?

Connecting to the Covenant

There is a covenant of greatness that has been given to our fathers passed down to us through the blood of Jesus. We know now that we have access to the Father, that we do not come into His presence with trembling lips and a fearful heart.

The covenant we have in Christ has done much more than giving us access. Age-long blessings that the Lord God swore to our fathers have now been unlocked for us to enjoy. We have been made heirs by faith in Him. Remember that we have the forgiveness of sins through Christ Jesus. Likewise, our names have changed. You are now the redeemed of the Lord, adopted into His sonship.

Thus, with every blessing that the Israelites walked in, we also have access. If we ponder on God's journey with the Israelites, we would see that our God is the sufficient God. Did you know that the Israelites had the best of it all? The choicest of jewelry, the best meals, enough wealth to build a gold-plated tabernacle. With God, there was more, and even more.

All this because God had made a covenant with their fathers. He was to them the God of Abraham, the God of Isaac, and the God of Jacob. And so, for we who believe, we have the freedom to walk into the realities of the same blessings that the Lord gave unto these people.

But then, you may say, nothing has changed about me. You have a job that only satisfies you on Friday afternoons. You have student loans to clear. Your body doesn't cooperate with your mind, and you find yourself succumbing to sickness, even when you would rather be healthy. Or perhaps, it's your family; everyone fights everyone, every time. It's as though there's always a fuse waiting to explode.

You may be thinking, "What's all the talk about the new covenant, the blessings of Abraham? I just need money to pay my mortgage and clear the loans I've taken. I just want a full week of not having to intervene in familial strife."

Although this covenant has been unlocked, you must be connected to its realities to have full access. Much like the laptop charger, the socket, and the laptop, you may have all the access to the blessings yet struggle to see them manifest in your life. Certainly, this is not God's intent for you or anyone around you. He intends that you prosper, that you be in good health, that the blessings of Abraham may play out in your daily affairs. What must you do then?

Believe.

If you are a child of God, you are already connected. This is the first step in your walk of faith. That you believe in the only begotten son of God. Galatians chapter 3 verse 9 says: *"So then those who are of faith are blessed with believing Abraham"* – GNT

Did you see that? So, if you are a person of faith, the Bible says that you are already blessed with faith like Abraham's. To be blessed with Abraham's faith is to journey from the confession of faith at the point of salvation to living each day in the faith-experience, doing all things by faith.

Connecting to the Covenant

There are many Christians who profess to be Christians, but they cannot live by faith. They live by the word of the world. They cannot do anything beyond their circle. They are afraid of everything. They are scared of themselves because they do not have faith.

To have faith is to come into a knowledge of the God you are serving. You must be able to commune with him, to take instructions from him. You cannot say that you have faith and you take instructions from the world. You cannot say that you have faith, and you take instructions from Google and Yahoo. Am I saying you should discard the internet and the resources contained therein? No way!

But you must realize that the bible is God's manual for living, handed to us. You must cultivate a habit of knowing what God says about a thing, as written in His word. For many of us, we wish that God would wave a wand and do a miracle in our lives.

"Oh, if only God would take away this cancer."

"I believe, I believe God can ask someone to send money into my account so that I can catch up on my outstanding bills. It's just so frustrating owing all these bills."

Do you see that? You can't claim faith and frustration in the same sentence. God honors His word, He responds to His word, His word binds him. Your faith in God is also proven by your faith in what God has said, even if at that moment, it makes no sense to believe it.

How often do we get emotional and teary when a minister makes a prayer of healing for a member, and the healing happens? Do you know how illogical it is to speak to someone who has a tumor that the tumor has melted? Indeed it doesn't conform to science. By science, when there's a tumor, you excise it. But not by God! Not by God!

If God would have that the sick person is prayed for, for the healing to occur, then prayer has to be the option we consider. I have heard several testimonies of people who believed in God for healing, for provision, for help, and as they sat to pray and read the word, they felt a tug to dance and worship. That was all they did. Just dance and worship. Does that make sense? By our thoughts, it doesn't.

Living in faith teaches us that God doesn't always do logic. You cannot say that you have faith and take decisions based on your bank account. Should you have a savings culture? Yes, you should. Should you be mindful of your income and expenditure? Yes, you should. But your approach must be one of faith; one that understands that the Father owns the silver and the gold, and not one born of fear, of worry, or of endless trepidation.

A lot of people have told me, "Pastor, what are you talking about! This faith is not easy." I am telling you that it is easy, but you have to believe in God. You must have a faith that will work for you because the blood of Jesus has made a way for you and me.

You say, "Oh, what if the faith doesn't work?" If it doesn't work, who is going to be put to shame? "Oh, everybody will laugh at me." If they laugh at you, why do you feel the shame? Because you are not yet dead to Christ. Because if you are dead to Christ, and you live for Him, whether they laugh at you or they don't laugh at you, it doesn't make any difference to you. Because it is not you that lives, it is Christ that lives in you.

That's why some of us struggle to pray for the sick, to believe God on behalf of someone in need of financial help. We would rather find a way to crowdfund the need or speak to someone who can help. We can't complain that our faith isn't "big" enough when we are unwilling to risk being foolish because that is not the way of the world.

We cannot even pray for ourselves to step out of our comfort zone because of fear. For a man of faith, if somebody says I am sick, he will say, "Come, let us pray." Because it is not you, you are not the healer. Who is the healer? God is the healer. You are just exercising your faith. So if you don't start praying for the sick, if you don't start praying for the bus to come on time so that you are not late for your appointment, if you don't start praying over a business proposal you received, if you don't start praying about the little things in your life, how can your faith grow so that you can live the covenant?

Let's look at Galatians 3 verse 26 to 29: *"It is through faith that all of you are God's children in union with Christ Jesus. You were baptized into union with Christ, and now you are clothed, so to speak, with the life of Christ Himself. So, there is no difference between Jews and Gentiles, between slaves and free people, between men and women; you are all one in union with Christ Jesus. If you belong to Christ, then you are the descendants of Abraham and will receive what God has promised."*

So, you see that this covenant does not depend on your color. It does not depend on the family you come from. It does not depend on the fact that you are free or slave. It does not depend on whether you have been successful or you've failed in the past. When you come into the covenant, you come to a leveled playground, where the principal currency is faith.

This is the only thing that gives us a leveled playground. This covenant is an opportunity for me and you to overtake our contemporaries, overtake our enemies, overtake our colleagues, and shine above those around us. This covenant pays little regard to where you come from. The only demand is that it be "by faith."

Whether you are in Africa, Canada, Haiti, everywhere, as long as it be, "by faith." In Nigeria, we say that a lizard in Nigeria cannot become a crocodile in Canada. A lizard will always be a lizard. Even if the lizard ventures from the grasslands of Ibadan to the Amazon forest, it will stay a lizard.

You know, we often talk about seeking greener pastures. But if you are a lizard inside of you, you will still be a lizard when you come to this country. Yet, if you were always a lion, you continue to grow as a lion immediately when you arrive in this country. The snow cannot stop you. The snow cannot stop anybody. Look at the sun shining; the way it shines here, it shines in Africa.

"Oh, this place is difficult, pastor, you don't understand."

Beloved, with and in God, faith is constant. In Canada and any geographical location, faith opens doors in God. God would not say, "Oh, you're in Ontario now. You need to switch your mode of faith."

No, beloved! So, do you believe? Have a culture of hard work!

Romans, chapter 12, verse 11: "Work hard and do not be lazy. Serve the Lord with a heart full of devotion."

Connecting to the Covenant

You know, when I gave my life to Christ, I loved this scripture. This was in the days while I was still in the university as a student. Back then, some people presented their studies as an excuse for not sustaining a fellowship with God. "I am writing for my exam. I do not have time for God," they would say.

There was the other set, too, those who had made the fellowship center their habitation but could never be caught studying. These two categories are wrong. As a believer, your walk with God does not disrupt your work. Because you do not stop being a believer when in class or at the office. Why, then, should one affect the other?

As I gave my life to Christ, I wanted to join the prayer team. They said I would have to present my transcript before I could be inducted. They look at your grades because they do not want you to blame God for your failures. So, the leaders said, "we don't want you to blame your academic performances, your all-around wellness, on God because you are serving God."

So, the leaders gave me this scripture, and since then, I have memorized it; "Not slothful in business; fervent in Spirit; serving the Lord." So, you cannot say because I am doing Church work, I cannot do anything else in other areas. I cannot take my exams; I am so busy; that is why I cannot serve God. It says, "not slothful in business."

So, you see, to connect to the covenant, as long as you are very busy, making money or other things, you still have to be strong in the Spirit by serving God. You have to find balance if you want to be connected, or you will never be connected.

The Blood Covenant

When Jesus was fasting for 40 days, after the fast, the devil went to him and said, "Jesus, I know you are starving. Take this stone and turn it into bread. I know you can do it. Just turn it into bread." And Jesus said, "Man shall not live by bread alone. But from every word that cometh out of the mouth of God." And I asked a brother, I said, "what does that mean to you?"

Many of us believe that the job we do or the business, or the money we make is what we live by. It is a mistake, and I will tell you why. If we wake up in the morning and you lose oxygen, will you be able to go to work? No, you will call 911. You will go to the hospital.

I met a guy last week. What was his problem? He cannot coordinate his mind and his speech. He was healthy, but you cannot pick up what he is talking about. Afflicted in the mind, he couldn't work. I ask, who is sustaining you? It is the Lord! That's why if you lose your job today, you will still be alive. But if God steps out of your situation today, you're done.

When you want to make decisions, when you read that scripture, how Jesus replied to the devil, you have to ask yourself, "What is more important to me?"

We say, "Man shall not live by bread alone," and then we go the length of a week without reading our bibles. But you eat every day from Monday to Sunday, don't you? Thank God for food. Even for those with bible apps on their phones, reading becomes the most challenging thing to do. Some of you will say, "Pastor, it is a tiny thing." But it shows your priority.

If you are not hardworking, you do not have a culture of hard work, and you cannot be connected fully to God's covenant. I believe when we begin to see our work – our jobs, our duties as husbands, wives, children, siblings, our businesses – as assignments from God. We understand the need to achieve synchronization between our faith journey and our physical businesses.

Do you know what a culture of hard work is? Maybe you don't. Maybe you do. I have seen a lot of people who do not understand what a culture of hard work is. We are not talking about "move this chair!" and you move the chair. When you see a man that has a culture of hard work, if he says, "I will pick that basket," nothing can stop him. If he says this year, this is what I want to do! If the law says they cannot do it, they will change the law to do it.

You know I love our white brethren; have you noticed our white brethren here? Oh! I love them for that! They don't take no for an answer. They will write articles in the paper; they will make calls to make sure that the law is changed. They will use any ways you can think of so that they make sure things work their way.

What about you and me? You know we Christians; you know what we say? Immediately there is an obstacle; we say, "it is not the will of God." We associate obstacles as warnings from God for us not to do a thing without searching His mind to know what He would have us do. It is improper to relegate a thing as not being the will of God because of obstacles. Moving forward is the will of God! Amen! How can something that will move you forward not be the will of God?

Recently, I was preaching in church, and I said, "Laziness fosters pettiness. Petty people also turn out to be lazy. They notice the slightest displeasing acts. They're the ones ignored during meetings; they're the ones not greeted. In this church, I don't know who greets me or who does not greet me because I know where I am going, and most times, when you know where you are going, it is only the people who share with you that vision that will greet you. So, if you don't know where you are going, you will carry a lot of wagons, both necessary and unnecessary." Do you know where you are going? A man who knows where he is going is not petty. Amen!

As a people of faith, people joined with Christ, we learn diligence in the Kingdom. Whatever your hand finds doing, you do it as though God spoke to you in a dream and asked you to report to Him. This was the nature Joseph carried in Egypt, the nature Jacob carried as he tended his in-law's flock, the character that David wore through his journey from shepherd to king. Diligence. A culture of hard work helps us lay hold of the realities of the covenant we have in Christ.

Obedience to biblical instructions.

In a later chapter, I write extensively on the necessity of a believer's total obedience, taking cues from biblical experiences. What inspired these people to fully heed what God was asking them to do?

Obedience eases your connection to God's covenant as a believer. In Isaiah 1:19, we find the blessings that come with obedience. *"If you will only obey me, you will eat the good things the land produces."*

Connecting to the Covenant

If you are willing and obedient, Canada will work for you. You know people believe all kinds of myths about this land. But I believe this is the best country in the world. This is the best country in the world where you can be a millionaire. This is the best country in the world where your children can experience healthy growth and increase because all the legislations, the laws, and everything else favors you. But if you are of faith and you believe God, and you are hardworking, if you have this culture of hard work, if you are obedient, then you will experience progress.

As believers, obedience to God teaches us to obey authorities. God doesn't breed rebels, hallelujah! One who is faithful in God's work would not refuse to pay taxes. It doesn't work that way with God.

What God is working in you, no one can stop it, except you give them room to do such. The covenants of God – of multiplication, of greatness – is in you already. You come from a lineage of people who did exploits in God. You have 'legal' access to many covenanted blessings. All you need to do is to believe God.

THE GENERATIONAL CONSEQUENCES OF A COVENANT

The history of the Israelites is one that does not cease to amaze me and should surprise you as well. I believe that one cannot accurately engage the Bible in a study without running into something that leads to the Israelites.

But consider how the Israelites came to be. We can trace the history in diverse ways. If you're particularly the scholarly type, you might find yourself immersed in the most accurate detailing of the Israelites' experience. Still, it's safe to agree that the story begins with Abraham.

The account opens with an instruction the Lord passes to Abram, to *"leave your country…your father's home…to a land that I am going to show you…I will bless you…that you will be a blessing." (Genesis 12: 1-2, NKJV)*

This simple communication between the two parties becomes the earliest established covenant between the Lord and Abram.

As we earlier established, the elements of a covenant are highlighted in this exchange. There are specific descriptions of the duties Abram is to perform and what God would bring to pass upon the performance of those instructions. As we read further, we see Abram's fulfillment, to the tiniest detail, the duties required of him. As the Sovereign God, the Lord would go on to establish His word with Abram, first giving him laughter in a child, Isaac, bringing forth Jacob, who introduces us to the people of Israel.

The Generational Consequences of a Covenant

Many times, we find ourselves, unwilling participants, to covenants that predate our existence. Given our birthplace, origin, tribe, parenting, or even upbringing, we are tossed into situations that are not of our own doing. We grow up into the agreements binding these covenants. We find out that our lives seem to play according to a script we didn't agree to, and on investigating, we are shocked to learn that a deal had been agreed to on our behalf.

When God makes a covenant with you, He doesn't stop with you, but He extends it to those coming behind you. Some of the experiences you have are results of what came before you, the agreements your predecessors had with a particular group of people.

In North America today, their forefathers were Christians. They served God. They went to Africa to preach to my forefathers, who were worshiping idols. And God prospered their children. Their children became prosperous, and they built everything that we see around us. But those children did not commit the realities of the covenant to their children, so by the time we came to North America, those children's children had left the foundation of this country.

There continues to be an increase in the desire to do only things that are convenient for them. Churches started to close down, and God said, what are we going to do? And I am sure that is why God brought you and myself to North America, to point people back to the light. If you have listened to the news over the past six months, you will be shocked at the degree of atrocities gaining ground in our cities.

The Blood Covenant

Do you know the atrocity with influence now? Drug overdose. You know I was just thinking about it, how do you explain it? Imagine two parents and their kids, all high on cocaine. To the extent that the 911 emergency team had to rush over to revive them. Ridiculous indeed!

Also, imagine this: In Vancouver, Canada, fifty people were treated for an overdose within one hour. It is hard to comprehend, but stories like these happen every day all over the world.

The power of covenants. That is the power of covenant. The generation where their fathers were transgressing the covenant, oh, they thought everything was okay. "Oh, I can do everything in my life! What are they talking about in church? The God that we do not see? Please pay no attention to this grandpa. He is just wasting his time with God."

Brethren, if you look at the statistics, you will see that everything they touched prospered because of that grace, that covenant with the fathers of this land because they gave their lives for the Gospel. But when the children of their children's children began to transgress, we found ourselves here today. You are a man under authority, and for this reason, you cannot do what you wish or live as you want. Praise the Lord.

The Church is the pillar of light. In this present day, God desires to establish the covenants He made with our forefathers in us. His words unto us are for us and unto a thousand generations after us. There are several blessings in scriptures that we can access as believers if we give attention to the conditions that bound them. God is in the business of fulfilling age-long blessings.

The Generational Consequences of a Covenant

In Nigeria, we are staunch believers in the generational effects of a covenant. For many of us, our childhoods were diffused with warnings from parents and elderly ones on the must-dos and must-not-dos we needed to observe, with a good portion of these being results of agreements our predecessors had made between themselves and even with deities.

I know of families where the male children suddenly contract strange sicknesses and die at forty. Without cause, without reason, without prior warnings. For others, marriage becomes a war with no light at the end of the tunnel. They struggle and strive before they get married, only for the marriage to experience the greatest of conflicts in the earliest months.

When these people come into Christ, they come under the influence of a new covenant, sealed by the blood of Jesus Christ. There begins a deliberate displacement of the consequences of whatever agreement bonded them to their predecessors. Deliberate because the terms of covenants are always honored. As such, if their predecessors had agreed to some worrisome conditions in time past, the consequences are bound to be manifested in these individuals.

But God is faithful. God is faithful. He is full of righteousness and truth, peace, and justice. He's eager to bring to pass the blessings we have by faith in Abraham because we are "heirs according to the promise."

What promise? The promises (covenants) between God and Abraham. Remember that these covenants were predicated on faith? It goes then that whosoever believes, has faith in God can enter into the blessings of Abraham. Abraham's blessings are indeed yours!

Looking at the nation of Israel, we see a heavy influence of the disciplines practiced by their forefathers, as far back as Abraham. About 2.3% of the country's GDP stems from agriculture, which only points back to patriarchs like Isaac, who sowed in the land and reaped a hundredfold in the same planting year (Genesis 26:12). Israel is one of the world's leading greenhouse-food-exporting services, exporting more than $1.3 billion annually.

Their agricultural sector alone employs about 1% of the entire population. Their main crops are fruits and vegetables, and cereals, as well as cattle farming. The Old Testament documents the accounts of several patriarchs who were successful both in agriculture and in animal rearing. They operated under the blessings of God, relying on the covenants God made with Abraham and those who came after him.

From these, we realize that "the apple doesn't fall far from the tree." Covenants are structured to affect even generations coming. How are you channeling the blessings of the covenants you're connected to?

ACCESSING THE BLESSINGS OF COVENANTS

The blessings of God's covenants are eternal. God does not desire that any of His children (for anyone who believes in the name of God is brought into sonship) miss out on His eternal purposes. Often, we become super interested in the earthly blessings contained in the written word that we forget that as our God is eternal, so are His blessings for us.

In the faith-based drama, 'Do You Believe?' After a chance encounter with a street preacher lugging a cross, Pastor Matthew reexamines his convictions about the cross of Jesus Christ and his commitment to preaching the truth to his church. Meanwhile, he and his wife were unable to conceive a child and found themselves in a situation to help a pregnant woman. While they struggled with the decision to provide shelter for the woman, Matthew shared a message about the cross with the congregation.

Countless times, we are overwhelmed by material needs that we lose sight of the blessings God has provided for us in His word. Even more, we are unskilled to enter and walk in the reality of these blessings. We read what the Bible says, yet it becomes a mystery for us to take these things from the scriptures into our realities.

Anyone who believes in the name of Jesus as the Lord is already blessed by God. This blessing is freely given to us by the Father. Ephesians 1:3 says that God has *"blessed us by giving us every spiritual blessing in the heavenly world."* Once we believe, the condition remains that we stay in

Christ – in all our endeavors, in every moment – and as we do, we are made partakers of blessings, spiritual and otherwise.

God does not desire that we be in want. King David, whom the Bible describes as a man after God's own heart, was one who understood that God's intent is our prosperity (see Psalms 23:1). Truly, when we make the Lord our shepherd and continually remind ourselves of His Lordship over our lives, we position ourselves to receive daily doses of blessings from Him.

We must learn the principles involved in accessing the blessings that God has designated for us, His people. How do we approach the presence of God through Christ Jesus to enjoy all that He has designed for us?

There was a story about a minister I read on the internet a while back. As the pastor of a large, faith-based organization, his daily schedule involved meetings, visits, and several other obligations. But the minister would separate an hour to be alone in his office, during which he would commune with God. The office staff knew not to fix a meeting for that afternoon hour or allow anyone into the office.

Once, the minister's daughter, five years old at the time, returned from school and headed for her father's office. As expected, the daughter was denied access. The minister would not like to be disturbed, the secretary said, and the daughter was asked to wait an hour until her father was done.

And what did she do? She nodded at the secretary's words, put her fingers on the door handle, and turned the knob. She strolled into the office before the secretary could react. Panicked, she jumped after the girl who was now in her father's arm, and she was surprised to meet the minister smiling, patting the child's hair.

What's the lesson for us? We are God's children, God's people redeemed by the blood of the Lamb. We do not tremble and quake in fear as we approach the presence of the Father. Through the giving of His only begotten Son, God gave us access to come directly into His presence.

Do you think God gave His Son so that we can wear FANCY clothes and head to church on Sundays and sing hymns and give our offerings and pray for ten minutes? Certainly not! Christ came to do much more than that. Much more!

You have life eternal in God. You have perfect health and wellness in God. You have wisdom, help, favor, a sound mind, a heart full of love, a mind blessed with God's power and strength. Great and precious promises are yours in Christ Jesus.

When you commit your life to Jesus Christ, you don't just get the blessing of a fancy house or a promotion at work, or success in the scholarship exams you're writing, or money for your next trip. Does God care about these things? Verily! Does God bless us with material things? Certainly! Does He bless us with much more? Yes, He does!

You have all-time, all-paid access to the Father. It's a very, very VIP ticket to all the shows and games, an invitation to partake of it all. The next three chapters are dedicated to examining three covenants in operation in the life of a believer. These covenants are instrumental to God's work in your life. If you only unlock their realities, you will come into much more fullness than you imagined possible.

I want you to know that God's spirit is in you, His power is at work in you. But often, we limit what God wants to do in our lives by our choices.

We have a foundational problem that we must correct. Some of us knew God as early as teenagers in Sunday School, and we've been made to believe God is a strict class teacher who walks about with a register for marking all our wrongdoings. So, someone says to us, "God's power is at work within you; you have the blessings of God." And we think to ourselves, "If only you know the things I've done. I'm not as innocent as I look. I've made terrible mistakes. God cannot forgive me. Heck, I wouldn't forgive me if I were God."

Can I say to you, thank God you're not God? Yes, God alone is God because He alone fully comprehends the character of God. The Bible tells us His thoughts are higher than our thoughts, His ways higher than our ways (Isaiah 55:8–9). There's nothing pleasant about being held under the weight of guilt, an unforgiving spirit, or a willingness to move on from a mistake.

I want us to examine some of the things that can hinder us from receiving the blessings of God's covenants.

Guilt

Sam was visiting his grandparent's big farm, where he loved to take walks and practice his shooting with a slingshot. He wasn't very accurate, and so he was content with shooting at cans and trees. Once, at the end of a walk, he spotted his grandmother's duck and decided to try his hand for the fun of it.

The Blood Covenant

Of course, he did not expect to hit the duck. He was still terrible with the slingshot. But when he released the stone, it struck the duck right in the head, killing it instantly. Sam didn't know what to do. He'd never hit anything before. Terrified, he carried the duck and buried it behind the farm's barn. Returning to the house, he spotted his sister, Julie, and knew immediately that she'd witnessed everything. Now there was a secret. Later that night, after dinner, his grandmother asked Julie to help with doing the dishes. "Grandmother," Julie said, right back, "I'd love to, but Sam said he would love to do the dishes tonight." As she headed out, she whispered to Sam, "Remember the duck." And she was gone.

The next morning, their grandfather invited the kids to go fishing, but their grandmother wanted Julie to stay back and help her with some chores. Again, Julie said, "Sam said he would love to stay with you and help you out with the chores." And as she left, she whispered again, "Remember the duck." This routine continued for a few days, with Sam tackling both portions of their chores until he decided to confess to his grandmother. And what did she do? Did she hit him in the face for hurting her precious little animal? She gave him a big hug.

She knew. She'd been at the window the evening the incident happened, and she'd seen how shocked the boy was at the turn of events. She forgave him at that moment, not holding any grudge, and she'd been watching to see how long he would allow Julie to make a slave of him for a crime he'd been forgiven of. Does this remind you of someone you know? A friend, a sibling, or even yourself?

God doesn't do guilt. The accuser of the brethren is not God or the Holy Spirit. The devil is the accuser of the brethren. You know, people have said to me, "I just felt horrible after I lied. It was like the Spirit of God was making me see how bad what I did was."

No, dear. God's Spirit doesn't tug you towards guilt but towards repentance. Give it some thought. God is willing to receive even the worst of sinners if they would confess Jesus as Lord. How much more you who believe in the resurrection and life, who has the Spirit of God resident in him, whose access to the Father is sealed by the blood of Jesus? *"There is no condemnation now for those who live in union with Christ Jesus." (Romans 8:1)* You do not have condemnation in Christ. God's spirit doesn't condemn but instead convicts towards repentance.

You have to say to yourself, "You know what? I shouldn't have done that, but I did. I confess my wrongdoing, and confess that Christ Jesus died for my sins, that God is faithful and just to forgive and cleanse me from all unrighteousness."

Once you do, you let go of the guilt. God doesn't do gradual pardon or probative forgiveness. You know, I'll give her 50% forgiveness and see if she would behave accordingly, or if she would go on causing trouble, making wrong decisions again. No, not God! So, you must walk with God here. God lets go of it, and you must let go of it all as well.

Unforgiving Spirit

Unforgiving spirit anchors us to the ship of guilt. Guilt breeds on our reluctance to forgive ourselves for our mistakes, errors, or wrongdoings.

You say, "I'm just bad, bad, bad. I just don't know how to do the right thing, even though I always want to, I always want to."

You change that confession. Say to yourself, "I am forgiven of the Lord. I have the righteousness of God. I have the peace of God. God gives me wisdom liberally, so I make the right decisions at all times, I do the will of God."

Our ability to forgive ourselves tell on how easily we forgive others. You cannot receive God's blessings in a heart wrapped in unforgiveness.

A man once went to the hospital for a random checkup. After reading his temperature, his doctor said asked if he had felt any symptoms recently.

"A little headache," the man said. "I've had struggles with sleeping."

"Well," the doctor said, "I'm going to give you a little sedative, and you'll sleep for a few hours. Is that fine?"

Sure, the man said. So, the doctor hooked him up and had him sleeping in no time. A few hours later, the man woke up. As expected, the headache was gone. "Never felt better," said the man, chuckling.

The doctor frowned. He'd rechecked the man's temperature, and this time it'd gone up a few degrees. Convinced the man wasn't showing any symptoms, the doctor asked, "By chance, do you have unforgiveness in your heart?"

Unforgiveness is like a boiler that doesn't go off. When you choose to hold on to grudges, when you choose not to forgive wrongdoings (yours or others), you emit an atmosphere that tinker with the fulfillment of God's blessings in your life.

Jesus said we should forgive our brothers "up to seventy times seven." That's four hundred and ninety times, enough to go around the year if you used one per day. That's how much God doesn't welcome unforgiveness in His Kingdom. You also shouldn't!

THE COVENANT OF MULTIPLICATION

God's system of operation tends towards the unreal. It defies logic. His ways are always past finding out. When God says a thing, He expects that we are fully persuaded that He can do what He has promised.

Multiplication is a principle that exists in God. From childhood, we are taught that specific rules guide arithmetic. For example, if you take three and multiply it by eight, your output would be twenty-four (24) under arithmetic laws. The only exception, one would expect, would be when operating under a different base number. Base numbers allow for tweaks in arithmetical processes, such that in base seven, eight multiplied by three equals thirty-three (33).

The everyday mathematics world runs on decimal, a base of ten (10), base ten dates as far back as 3000BC, evidenced by Egyptian hieroglyphs. There are many proponents as to the cause for the adoption of ten as the conventional base number. One says that we are blessed with ten fingers, so it's only natural to count in tens, hence, base ten.

Now, I want you to imagine a boy of seven or eight. A typical child raised in a natural environment, not a future Sherlock Holmes. At that age, you probably knew the multiplication tables up to six. I remember growing up, we would recite the tables every weekday before and after breakfast. The faster you could gobble up those numbers, committing them to memory and recalling without mistake, the more praise was showered on you.

The Covenant of Multiplication

So, you have a seven-year-old boy learning that nine multiplied by four is thirty-six. The tables prove so. The boy believes so. He's spent half an hour daily for the last school term learning this. You could wake him from sleep, and he would deliver the same answer to you. Let us assume the boy's friend, Joe asks him to come for a sleepover. Sleepovers are known to improve bonding between kids, right?

The boy goes for a sleepover, and right before the boys prepare for bed, Joe's father, who teaches mathematics at the community's high school, calls him to his study and asks him to recite the multiplication tables. The study is a compact room with a lone window, and the air is dense with tension. So, Joe crosses his arms behind him and begins to recite the tables, picking from fours and swinging into fives, sixes, and eights.

Our boy nods along. He knows the table. Only that, at a point, Joe switches to something the boy doesn't understand. Suddenly nine multiplied by four isn't thirty-six, but fifty-one. The boy looks towards Joe's father for a disapproving look but meets none. Seconds later, Joe makes another slip-up. This time, he says, twelve times four is sixty-six. The boy shrieks. Four times twelve is forty-eight. It's in basketball. Everyone knows that!

The mishap continues till the end of Joe's recitation, and Joe's father doesn't frown once. Later, in bed, the boy nudges Joe. What happened out there? Isn't twelve by four forty-eight? Isn't it? Joe, with a smile, says, "Oh, I was reciting them in base seven. My dad has been teaching me numerical bases, and that's a faster way to learn them." As believers, are we Joe? Or are we the boy?

In comparison, we could say that God operates under an infinite set of base numbers. Infinite because He's the Infinite God, existing before time, and as such, isn't bound by anything under time. Recall that we say, "A thousand years is like one day before God." Under the conditions of math, that is neither logical nor plausible. With God, nothing shall be impossible.

God has given us the covenant of multiplication. The covenant of multiplication grows a $10 business into a $10,000 business upon acting on God's word. When God blesses us, it is not to the end that we ride fancy cars. You know, we imagine God's blessings as being equal to a gated apartment, a swimming pool dug into the earth downstairs, a nice view of the skyline from the main bedroom's window. But it's more than that. Much more than that.

Pastor Kenneth Copeland, one of America's wealthiest pastors, recounts several instances where they received a burden to sow a portion of all they had to a ministry project. They acted in faith, believing that the word they had received was true, from God. And at every time, God always seemed eager to multiply that which they had already.

I know that our Father is much more interested in our prosperity than we can ever think ourselves to be. Just as He cares much more about our salvation, spirit, and soul than we do. You must approach the reality of multiplication with a meek heart, a heart that knows His sufficiency is in God and not in the wealth He has received of God.

The Covenant of Multiplication

Multiplying the wealth God has given unto us requires that we operate in divine wisdom and favor with both God and man. God is not carnal, and by extension, those who would rely heavily on the Spirit, who would walk in the Spirit (Ephesians 5:16) are not carnal either.

Interestingly, the word "carnal" is derived from the root word "sarkikos," and one of the meanings is to be "governed by mere human nature not by the Spirit of God." Carnality speaks to our dependence on our human systems, just as it speaks to the "idea of depravity in human."

Writing to the church in Corinth, the apostle Paul calls them carnal because there was among them, "Envy, jealousy, and strive."

Not fornication! Not drunkenness! Not cursing! We see from these that it is very much possible for the believer to be moral yet carnal. Any decision that doesn't stem from the Spirit, under God, is carnal.

Thus, our need for divine wisdom. As you seek to multiply that which God has given you, it must be done by the Spirit. What does this mean? It means that if the Spirit instructs that you work all night and all day during a particular season, your decision to take breaks would tend to carnality. If the Spirit says, "Give," then you must interpret the instruction as "give" and not "sow."

Joe and Mark worked as heads of divisions at a production company. Within a few months, they realized they were both believers, and a mutual friendship ensued. Not only that, their families were set up in similar fashions – one wife, three kids (two girls, a boy holding the middle). They spent the chunk of their free time together, talking faith, family, and certainly, finances. The obvious difference between the two was that Mark was two years older than Joe.

One afternoon, around the time that the company would reward heads of units with a commensurate bonus, the men went out to lunch. Mark raised the topic of their bonus and how he intended to sow a part of it towards a mission's ministry in Israel. He asked if Joe would do the same too.

Earlier that day, Joe was speaking with his wife when the bonus slipped into the conversation. His wife swiftly reminded him of the overdue trip to his parents' and how the bonus could come in handy since they wouldn't worry about the cost of traveling. Joe agreed. They made mental conclusions on the logistics.

Joe informed Mark he would think about the sowing. Mark pushed some more, reminding him of the sermon they'd heard a while back. The pastor had spoken on the need for more Christians to give to the work of the ministry, trusting that the blessings would circle back to them, for God would surely take care of His people.

Every morning till the bonus was paid to them, Mark would find Joe and whisper to him, "Have you decided yet?" Eventually, Joe took a portion of his bonus and sent it to the ministry, not consulting his wife.

Within a few days, the bonus had been disbursed towards unplanned needs, and the trip to their parents was postponed till December.

The Covenant of Multiplication

There are many Joes in the twenty-first-century church. Full of good works and intentions, but not subjecting ourselves to the leading of the Spirit in all things. Giving unto the work of the ministry is essential but giving when God would have you give is more essential. Not everyone would give to the work of the ministry. Some would give to the hungry and some to the orphans and widows.

I often ask myself, "What if the Good Samaritan had given all the money he had with him as an offering?" Of course, he was a Samaritan, and in our modern setting, he wouldn't be caught in a church service. But he could have driven by a beggar and given the wealth he had with him. What would have been the fate of the man robbed and maimed and left to die? How could the Samaritan have even known that God would need him to be of help to a wounded man?

We cannot always know what lies ahead. We need not worry too much about this. God knows more than we would, and so He asks us to trust in His wisdom, to trust in His Spirit, to walk in the Spirit.

Similarly, living in the reality of multiplication requires favor with God and man. When we have favor, multiplying the wealth God has given us becomes easy. Poverty will be kept far away from us.

The Bible says that, *"Ask of me, and I shall give thee the heathen for your inheritance, and the uttermost parts of the earth for thy possession" (Psalm 2:8)*. So, if God says we should ask of him, it means that He will give it to us. If He gives it to us, are we going to be able to manage it?

We pray, "Lord, prosper me, prosper me," but we have not developed the capacity to handle God's prosperity. I was reading about a Saudi prince who is a billionaire, and something caught my attention. I realized that this man sleeps only for 4 hours a day. Can you imagine that? This guy has businesses all over the world. In fact, by the time he left university at the age of 26, his father gave $30,000 and another $300,000 loan. When we left University, we did not have that kind of money. I thought the father would have given him 3 million dollars, but he gave $300,000 and $30,000 as a gift. This man multiplied this money and is today a multi-billionaire.

When I read that he sleeps only 4 hours a day, he works throughout the day until 4 a.m., and he is awake by 8 a.m. again. Praise the Lord! That's why the Bible says when men sleep, the enemy sow.

Ask yourself, how long do I sleep? There's a wonderful book I know, *The 5 am Club*, that I think every believer should read. The book highlights the benefits of being an early riser. You cannot be a custodian of God's blessings, of God's creation, and spend eight hours, ten hours sleeping every day. No, you have to get up and put yourself to work.

Reading the story of the Saudi prince challenged me. How much more should I do as a believer? We have examples for us in the scriptures. Isaac and his men dug wells upon wells upon wells. This was after he had reaped a hundredfold of his planting in one year. He'd become so prosperous that the Philistines in Gerar envied him and so sent him away.

He pitched his tent in the valley of Gerar and dug a well. The herdsmen came and claimed the water as theirs, so he moved further and dug another, and another, which he named Rehoboth. Imagine the efforts required to dig a well. I bet some of us would simply forget about the whole business, especially if you've just reaped a hundredfold harvest.

God says, "I shall give you the heathen for your inheritance." You pray to receive this inheritance. As you pray, you also ask for wisdom to know what to do, and how to do it, and for favor for every effort.

You need the wisdom to enjoy this covenant and every other covenant God has made with us. Wisdom is profitable in unlocking the covenants of fruitfulness. Likewise, with the covenant of prosperity – which we shall look at now –wisdom is crucial.

THE COVENANT OF PROSPERITY

Of the many things believers across different denominations do not have a unanimous agreement about, money ranks high. We do not like to talk about money. We think money and conversations about it are somewhat inconvenient, tainted with grime. We believe that God frowns when we gather to pray, and we ask for financial blessings. If our pastors happen to preach a sermon on prosperity, then suddenly they are "backsliding." Countless prominent ministers have come under heavy criticism given their stance on prosperity and why every believer should live a prosperous life.

But if we would consider the Bible as our standard for living, and we certainly should, then, we must be willing to talk about money the way God would have us engage the subject.

Christian history is filled with the experiences of people who had more than enough. The apostle Paul, the author of thirteen epistles in the New Testament, gave several admonitions on why any believer who doesn't work shouldn't eat. Even with the extreme demands of his ministerial assignments, he was a tentmaker. Luke, who documented the gospel of Luke and the accounts contained in Acts, was a doctor. Not only was he skilled in medicine, but it is also suggested that Luke was a rich man writing to a rich "most excellent Theophilus."

God doesn't intend in any way that the believer lacks money. While we do not forsake the seeking of righteousness for money, we must admit that God has blessed us with all blessings, and our finances are not excluded. God desires to bless the works of our hands. God desires to breathe into our businesses and make us prosper.

Remember King David? The man who played harp unto God, who danced to the Lord God with no degree of restraint? The man who was called a man after God's own heart. Here's what he writes: *"…how great is the LORD, He is pleased with the success of his servant." (Psalm 35:27)* The King James version introduces the word "prosperity" for "well-being."

We must believe that God is pleased when we are prosperous. When we work, God wants to bless the works of our hands. When a need arises to be met, God wills that we would have more than enough to abound. That is His desire. We should then ask, what does it mean to be prosperous? How can I key into the covenant of prosperity established in scriptures? Well, look at Genesis 26:13, and begin at verse 12. *"Isaac sowed crops in that land, and that year he harvested a hundred times as much as he had sown because the LORD blessed him. He continued to prosper and became a very rich man."*

You see, the Bible says that the man waxed great. He moved forward. What a statement! What a record! To have it said of you, "He moved forward until he became very great." It says, and he went forward and grew until he became very great. That is a covenant being confirmed in the life of Isaac. Isaac was not present when the Lord sealed this covenant with Abraham, but being Abraham's offspring, he became a partaker of it. This is our present-day reality too. The covenant of prosperity hangs over us, and so we must jump to catch it.

The Blood Covenant

Suppose you were born into a family where farming was the tradition. Your early years would be invested in learning the ropes, agriculture, and the business acumen needed to earn success in trading farm products. You do this for ten, twenty, thirty years, working with and under your father.

And then your father passes away, and the farmlands are transferred to you. By now, you are equipped with the know-how, but you may decide to stay away from the farm to seal it off because you're scared to toe the line your father cleared. You may move on to other businesses, only visiting the farm once yearly, in memory of your father.

Your decision to continue the cultivation of the inherited farmlands doesn't affect your ownership of it. You can be in ownership of a thing yet not enjoy the benefits of that thing.

The covenant of prosperity is knitted into our existence in the Kingdom. But that you have it does not mean you would operate in it or that you would manifest it. The wise man wrote in Proverbs, *"Through wisdom is a house built, and by understanding it is established…" (Proverbs 24:3).*

You then ask, "As a covenant-carrier, how can I manifest it?" Wisdom! God releases unto us the wisdom we need to walk in these covenants. He says to you, "Open your hands wide, allow me to pour my wisdom into you. Come on, don't cup those hands. Open them wide."

How does the wisdom of God help us operate the principles that unlock the reality of prosperity? We will look at two words that speak a lot about the operation of wisdom.

The Covenant of Prosperity

The first word is "make." To make is to create, to beget, to generate, to accomplish, to produce, to prepare, to institute. Make originates from the root word "asah." It captures God's intention when He made man. *"Let us make man…"* God was saying, "Let us institute a new system that has never been seen, the system of man."

To be great, you need the wisdom of God to generate unique ideas. Amen! You and I need God's wisdom to create unique ideas to make things happen for us. God's wisdom inspires us towards genuineness, towards a form of creativity that can amaze the world and those around us. The Spirit of wisdom is a fundamental expression of God's Spirit, and one way we know we walk in this wisdom is our ability to be ingenious.

Look at Jacob in the house of Laban. Laban was a shrewd man, a fraud of a businessman. And Jacob? Jacob was an enamored man. Jacob loved Rachel, and he was willing to go all-in for her. Love would make you do what you never considered yourself willing to do.

You know the story. Jacob was in that house, and he served Laban for seven years so he could marry his daughter, Rachel. Then Laban defrauded him by giving Jacob Leah, Rachel's elder sister, claiming that the elder must be married before the younger. So, Jacob worked for another seven years, for a total of fourteen. The man gave him Rachel and then told him, "Look, I don't want you to go; name your wages, and I will pay you if you continue to serve me."

This was a ridiculous suggestion. Recall that Jacob had been with him for fourteen years, so he could marry his heartthrob. Then he stayed with him as his wives began to conceive, first Leah, and then Rachel, for another period of fourteen years. In all this, Jacob did not take any wages for himself. And when the time came for him to leave, his uncle was unwilling to release him.

Thank God for His unique wisdom. When God gives you unique wisdom, it will make things happen for you. That is the covenant working inside of you. Every time you look at yourself and cannot get out of any challenges, any problem, you need to cry for God for wisdom.

I am sure Jacob must have looked up and said, "Let me go and think about it!" Amen! By the time he came back, he said to Laban, "Here's the wage I ask. Give me three days with your flock. Afterward, any speckled animal would be mine, and any animal without speckles will be yours."

Laban must have thought, "Oh well, the speckled animals are weak and ready to die. This man, Jacob, will spend a long time serving me, and he doesn't even know it yet."

What Laban did not know was that Jacob was a man under a covenant. Jacob himself may not have realized it at that time, but God's wisdom was nudging him towards creativity. Often, we think that our enemies are only those who do not like us. A person in your own family can be an enemy, even your advisor, that person you run to for advice, can direct you to another way outside of God's will. But thanks be to God for the wisdom of God. By His wisdom, we know all things, and we walk in all things.

As soon as Jacob departed the presence of Laban, the wisdom of God swung into action. God laid it upon his heart to modify the water troughs that fed the flock. Consequently, as they came to drink, they conceived, and the flocks which came were all speckled, streaked, and spotted. That is genetic engineering at its finest. At the end of twelve years, Jacob had more cattle and sheep than Laban. In twelve years. The wage of fourteen years was paid in the balance of twelve years, to the extent that the sons of Laban began to be jealous.

Do you see what the covenant can do? Jacob could have protested physically; he could have tried to fight for himself, but he went to God, and that's why we are here today. More than acquiring knowledge on what to do, we need the wisdom of God to teach us how to go about doing what we need to do.

We know that place that we have read in Genesis. Isaac, the father of Jacob, you know what he did in the land of the Philistines? The Bible says there was famine, he wanted to run to Egypt, but God told him not to go. So, he decided to stay with the Philistines' land, and the Bible says he dug well. There were so many problems, and when he dug the well, the Philistines closed it.

The digging stopped when Isaac came to the valley. The valley is the place where nobody wants to go. It is unsuitable for agriculture. But the Bible said that he dug there, and he hit a spring of water, and he kept the well. The Philistines did not want to go and pursue him there. And the Bible said that he sowed in that land, and it yielded a hundred folds. And that's why it says: *"He continued to prosper and became a very rich man. Because he had many herds of sheep and cattle and many servants, the Philistines were jealous of him." Genesis 26:13*

People say that what happened here was that when he dug the well, he got to a spring of water, and from that spring of water, he developed the first irrigation system to water for all the land. Do you see the importance of ideas? Do you see the importance of wisdom? As we pray, asking God for wisdom, we follow up with actions.

You pray, "God leads me to the well that will be enough for my family, even generations after because we are children of the covenant." The enemy can't stop you, and you can move for days until you find yourself in a place where nobody can trouble you. In that place where no one can trouble you, there is a spring of well there waiting for you to discover.

Brethren, we talked of the spring of well; it might be your career because nothing is permanent when God leads you to a spring of well. You see, when he dug the first well, the Philistines came and closed it. Then he dug the second one, and he kept digging until he got to the spring of water, there for him. That was where his greatness started. And similar to Jacob, the Philistines envied him. God will bless you with such an immense blessing that will make your enemy envy you in Jesus' name.

The second word is "manage." Brethren, we must have the wisdom to manage the idea that God has given to us. You see, if God gives you an idea and you don't do anything about it, because of fear of failure or because of your concern at what people would say, since everyone is doing it, then nothing would change about your situation.

Look at Mark Zuckerberg today, the co-founder of Facebook. That man is a billionaire today just because of an idea, and you know he was not the originator of that idea. The idea began with a set of twins, also

Harvard students. They came from a wealthy background, and they had the resources to execute the idea. They hired Zuckerberg as a programmer and planned to pay him $1,000 to help them write the program, but these people did not know the potentials of their idea.

The project was to allow them to communicate with their friends within the campus. They wanted to implement a social network. And it was the idea that Mark Zuckerberg expanded to create Facebook. Upon seeing the potential of their idea, the twin sued him, claiming that he stole it. Actually, the twins gave it to him based on the agreement they signed. The twins said that the deal was no more relevant because the idea became big money.

They came away from the suit with about half a billion dollars (not sure now). And they started another start-up. Do you see why effective management of ideas is important? Instead of Mark, it could have been those twins we would be talking about today.

When you have an idea, it is God that has placed it there. Don't kill it! You know, at that time, nobody knew anything about social networking. The technology was not even there. I am just telling you that we carry ideas, and most of us don't do anything with them. How many ideas come into your head? Even if there is no technology to pursue it, you can unpack it, and when the time comes, the technology will catch up.

Because if you make things happen, you must ready yourself to generate ideas that transcend trends or normality. The Bible doesn't tell us of anyone else who modified drinking water to produce streaked animals. Jacob could have hesitated with that idea. He could have chosen to stay content with the meager pay from his uncle, but the wisdom at work within him wouldn't let him.

How often do you engage the wisdom of God in your doings? Are there areas of your life that are off-limits to God? Could they be the choice of partners you date? Or the investments you make? Or the friendships you maintain? Let God shine the light on every area of your life and watch the transformation that would fill your every being.

As a church, we do not go about evangelizing with a lackadaisical attitude. It is no more business as usual; we have to generate ideas. One of such was our decision to create an online church community, such that people could be partakers of our services from wherever they were joining. So, all over the world, people are watching us. Ten years ago, it wouldn't have been possible. Those people cannot come here, but they are still partakers of the same services we partake of.

Brethren, what idea is God giving you? I remember when that idea first came up. The cost was so high that we did not even want to go there. I remember that one of our brothers made all kind of efforts to get this thing done, and I use that example because when they gave us the invoice, we said, "no, no, no! We are going to pray about it," but it was still in our heart, and when the opportunity came, we seized it. That is how you manage ideas.

It looks too big for you today does not mean that it will be impossible for you tomorrow. Because everything you need to make it happen, God will bring it your way. But if you change your mind like those twins who allowed Mark to prune the idea of Facebook off them, if you say I cannot do it now and you completely forget it, when the resources come your way, you will not remember to use it.

Do you see it now? You need to make a confession of God's wisdom at work in your life. An idea will lift you from poverty, and that idea is waiting to be implemented. God desires that you prosper. God wants that you are fruitful. The Lord Himself will grant you the wisdom to implement it in the name of Jesus.

THE COVENANT OF FRUITFULNESS

April brings with it the feeling of growth. The clouds are dense with rain, the streets strum as humans shuffle between work, school, and home, and the trees begin to sprout new leaves.

For farmers and agriculture enthusiasts, April is a month to anticipate. Before April, seeds are prepared, the land is tilled and allowed to regain nutrients, and the produce from the last planting seasons are sorted – stored, processed, stocked, transported, sold, consumed. Farmworkers take the gap between January – about the time the cold of early harmattan parts for the dusty atmosphere to settle – and March to observe, plan, strategize, and refresh. By the time the earliest rainfalls greet the paths, planting is ready to commence.

Planting in Nigeria shares many similarities with planting in any other country. Despite the glaring differences like the weather in different countries, some factors remain consistent. The land must be tilled. The seeds must be cast into the soil. The seeds must be watered regularly. Photosynthesis must take place, meaning any farmer hopes for an equal measure of sunlight and rainfall.

We can regard these guiding factors as laws, principles set in place to ensure commensurate returns on sowing. In Nigeria, there are two planting seasons for corn. Early planting occurs in March, and late planting occurs in July. On average, returns take four months to come around. This is subject to the degree of sunlight exposure, nutrient reception through the soil, and the planter's tending of the farmland. Hardly does a farmer plant without expecting that the seeds bring an increase.

In the Kingdom, we can equate this expected increase to God's expectation that we are fruitful as believers. It is amazing to discover that fruitfulness is pivotal to our experiences as Christians. If we want to be great, then we must be fruitful.

Once in a while, you may have conflicting thoughts that call out everything in your life that isn't working well. But you must realize that God is with you through every season. He is in you, He is with you, and He is for you.

God says to you, whenever you question if you have all it takes to be all that He has designed you to *"Have many children so that your descendants will live all over the earth and bring it under their control."*

There is no joy in saying I am Christian; I can speak in diverse tongues, and there is no progress in your life. There is no need because that doesn't glorify God whether you are a student, a businessperson, or a family member. It doesn't bring God glory, and God is big on glory. As Jesus walked the earth, He would often say, "…and glorify my Father in heaven."

This is why our light must shine so bright. That's why we must walk in the covenant of fruitfulness. It's not just about us having money but becoming a spring unto others.

I understand that sometimes barriers prevent us from living in fruitfulness. Sometimes those barriers are beyond us. Psalms 107 verse 34 says, *"He made rich soil become a salty wasteland because of the wickedness of those who lived there." So, the presence of wicked people in a fruitful land makes the land barren. Wickedness corrupts all forms of fruitfulness.* But it doesn't end there. In verses 35-36, the Bible says, *"He changed deserts into pools of water and dry land into flowing springs. He let hungry people settle there, and they built a city to live in."*

See how powerful God is, turning a wilderness into pools of water, to the end that the hungry may have sufficiency. That is God's business. Turning dry periods into seasons of fruitfulness, making abundance out of scarcity, that is God's desire.

There is a covenant of fruitfulness that God has given unto us. If you look at Leah and Rachel's case in Genesis 29: 31, the Bible says, because of the way she was treated, God opened the womb of Leah and closed the one of Rachel. It is God that closes and opens. He is the one that can make a fruitful land to become arid.

I always thank God for the country He brought us to. I believe strongly that the prayer of the people is a strong factor for all the marvelous works happening in Canada here. If people choose not to acknowledge God's working, nor give Him the honor due to Him, it costs God nothing to rewrite the affairs of that nation. Nothing.

When God blesses you, he expects you to appreciate Him for what he gave you. If you leave His presence and begin to do those things that are convenient for you. God can reverse the blessing. Genesis 29:31. It says:

"When the Lord saw that Leah was loved less than Rachel, He made it possible for her to have children, but Rachel remained childless."

The Covenant of Fruitfulness

You see that the Almighty God can open and close the womb, to favor or to punish. But if we continue to seek His mercy, He would bring us into the fulfillment of His covenant of fruitfulness. And we would not know barrenness.

What is the promise of God for us? Read Exodus 23:26. I often advise people to, "Take care of your children, bring your children to church, let them hear the Word of God, teach them about God, be consistent with God, and let them see you being consistent so that the covenant can continue with them." *"In your land, no woman will have a miscarriage or be without children. I will give you long lives." (Exodus 23:26)*

That is a promise. Deuteronomy 7:14 is another promise. *"No people in the world will be as richly blessed as you. None of you nor any of your livestock will be sterile."*

For fruitfulness, there is a seed of fruitfulness in you, but you have to be self-disciplined. You have to be obedient to God, and God must be assured that you are going to turn your children to him. But if you are the type who is fearful, if you are the type that does not know God, these promises are not for you.

The Jews represent 0.6% of the world population, but they control 26% of the world's wealth. It is amazing, amazing. You can go on and research it. There are many reasons for this, but at its core are the different covenants at work in their lives. They do not live ordinary lives. No! Not at all! Spiritually we are also Jews, by the blood of Jesus that was shed at Calvary, and by our adoption as sons and daughters of God. So, we should also be productive. Amen! Our community needs it. Our families need it.

Fruitfulness positions us in a state where we can add to others without reducing on our end. It goes beyond how much money we have to being vessels equipped to meet needs.

When you walk in the covenant of fruitfulness, you can speak blessings over the lives of people and have these blessings stand. You don't have to be a pastor, or a minister, to pray over situations and see these situations transform.

Joseph found himself in Egypt, but not by His own doing. He didn't desire it. His brothers had decided he was a threat and so sent him off to the household of Potiphar. The Bible records of him that God *"made all he did to prosper in his hands."* That's a level of fruitfulness that goes beyond what you have to what those around you also have.

Be mindful of being so focused on your desires and needs that you pay no attention to the needs of those around you. Sometimes, God would have you release a prayer into the life of a friend, a colleague, a neighbor. Your obedience to this would birth a season of much reaping in your own life.

You cannot fully comprehend the ways of God, so learn to be in tandem with God. Speak what He would have you speak. Listen to what He would have you listen to. Plant only when He instructs. Be still and be obedient. Be willing to add unto others, to be a blessing unto others. God is leading you into a season of fruitfulness, of much increase. Do you see it?

KNOWING YOUR IDENTITY IN CHRIST

One of the most riveting statements ever contained in a book is that made by Marianne Williamson in the book, A Return to Love. Since publication, the paragraph has appeared in different shapes and forms across varying cultures and geographical contexts. Marianne writes, "Our biggest fear is not that we are inadequate. Our biggest fear is that we are powerful beyond measure…We ask ourselves, "Who am I?"

At the core of the delivery is a question that challenges the reader to embark on a journey of reflection. Too often, we spend our days immersed in the survival chase that we allow only so little room for introspection. As such, when a statement comes sweeping in that calls to the innermost part of our essence, time stops, and our yearnings become pronounced.

Who am I? Who are you? Who does God say we are?

I recently encountered a presentation on identity by a writer who believes every human is constantly in a battle of self. He leads us into the story of Kent, the movie character that doubles as Superman. The bit about superheroes, the writer says, is that they're just like every other human. They sleep. They get hungry. They have to shower. They speak the same English governed by the same set of letters.

But then, Superman should not forget that beyond being Kent Clark, he's also superman, the guy with the cape. He could be facing a situation that demands him to step into the person of Superman but be powerless to do so. The moment he realizes that he's not just Kent, but also Superman, he can take on his cape and fly out and save the world.

What am I getting at? Superheroes continue to inspire us because we see a fragment of ourselves in them. We see Kent Clark and think, oh, how cool it would be to be Superman? We watch Peter do his spider-stuffs and imagine for a bit that we were Spiderman, zigzagging through alleys, shifting from one universe to another to stop a crisis, rescue the planet.

More than sources of inspiration, we should take these movies as a call to reach out to our true identity. And the right place to start searching is in the Bible. The Bible is God's manual that reveals unto us the entirety of who we are in Christ and what God has said about us.

Your identity in Christ is not black or white, Caucasian or Hispanic, Jew or Greek. Our generation has witnessed a lot of conflicts born out of our struggles with identity. We fight ourselves because we disagree with the labels others have placed on us. We feel a restriction on our rights, in our freedom.

But God doesn't relate with you based on the color of your skin. What is inside of you is more significant than how you look. I say the seed of God that is resident within you is greater than whatever label you have worn all your life.

Think about the immense people within your ancestry. As a believer, you have been inducted into the family of God, into the household of God's people. We have talked extensively about the covenants we share with Abraham through faith but think on it for a moment. Take a moment and consider it. Pace around your room if you must. Abraham left his family's house, a comfort zone, for a land God was to show him. By this, he received the covenants. That is faith in your lineage. Isaac obeyed the Word of God and sowed, and in the same year, he reaped a hundredfold. Such sacrifice and devotion bring fruitfulness and an increase in your lineage.

Joseph was made the head of the prisoners in Egypt. He interpreted Pharaoh's dreams and was made the Prime Minister of Egypt in those days. You have wisdom that confounds logic in your lineage. Deborah led the men of Israel to battle, and God gave them the victory. She sang a song of triumph to the name of the Lord. That shows courage in you and your history. Daniel was ten times better than his contemporaries. He was an excellent man who understood and interpreted dreams. During his days, he operated in the wisdom which comes from God. That's another portion of wisdom in your lineage.

Or what shall I say of David who slew Israelites' tormenter, Goliath, and triumphed over him? It shows strength in your lineage. Or of Moses, who parted the Red Sea, leading the Israelites out of captivity. Or Rahab, who hid the spies from Israel, receiving them with peace, by so doing saving her life and that of her family. Or of Gideon, who obeyed the instruction of the Lord and enjoyed an overwhelming victory.

Who are you? You are not a superhero. You are a son of the Most High God. You have His genes in Him. You are not mediocre. We often do not live in the completeness of who we are in Christ because it isn't trendy or cool.

Knowing your identity in Christ

You are not saved to be the next cool kid. Your lineage is made up of people who were not cool enough or likable enough but who knew what authority they had in them and whose name they lived.

You can only live in reality you've accepted as yours. You can't afford to settle for less or to undermine your abilities. God is always at work within you, but you must be willing to let Him furnish you unto the perfect man.

A Christian woman who worked at a fast-food outlet was always comparing herself to the customers who came to order food. "If only I had a fine car like that, I wouldn't be here packing donuts and burgers for a living," she would say. "I wish I had a fit body like this woman. Just see how fit she is. I bet she can do a hundred push-ups in one morning. I can barely get myself out of bed without feeling like I am carrying a mountain on my back. God, I wish I could trade places with her."

Don't give yourself over to such an attitude. The Bible informs that God is pleased with you. You have peace with God. You are beautiful, fearfully, and wonderfully made in His sight. This talks much more than about our physical bodies.

Of course, God cares about how we look, how we smell, the healthy nature of our meals, and a host of other things we crave for. But you shouldn't limit God's interests in your life to mere physical needs. You're much more than that.

Imagine David had said, "I can't fight this Goliath. I don't even look like a soldier. I'm just a rangy teenager who's good with the slingshot. Killing a Philistine isn't my business. What would my father even think?"

Did he think that? No. Instead, he remembered the experience he had with the lion and the bear, and he knew the same God who gave him victory over those would help him triumph greatly over Goliath. To this day, we refer to this wonderful experience, but we must realize that it took David to acknowledge the deposits of the Creator within him to face off Goliath.

God loves you immensely. God loves you tremendously. If we had a glimpse of how much God loved us, I believe we would spend every minute of every hour of every day single praises and worship to the Lord. We would continuously say, "Oh, for you are good, and your mercies endure forever. Oh, for you are great and greatly to be praised, in all the earth."

The righteousness you have before God and in God is sealed by the blood of Jesus Christ. Abraham believed God, and it was counted to Him for righteousness. You believe in the death of God's first begotten, and you become righteous before Him. You do not even have to leave your father's country and your father's house. Isn't that a glorious thing?

I'm not saying you are a finished work that needs no further furnishing. Certainly not. But your state in Christ is that of a perfect state. Each day is another opportunity for God to work in you until you become what He intends for you to be.

Would you make mistakes? Would you struggle in your walk with God? Would you struggle in your relationship with your fellow men? Would you take offense at displeasing situations? Would you have fallouts with your partner? Whenever you find yourself making mistakes, whenever your experiences fall short of God's design for your life, do not allow the devil to trap you with condemnation. Approach your Father's presence with the boldness of one whose sins are forgiven, and say, "Lord, I repent of all my wrongdoings. Help me to live according to your will. Amen!"

I have met several people who think the concept of a righteous standing with God is overblown. They go, "Yes, I know Christ died for my sins. But I think I'll just keep making mistakes anyway. I want to love the Lord and be a good person, but I just keep doing bad, keep hurting people, and doing silly things."

Well, brethren, I have news for you. You're not to be a good person. You're to be a God-person—God's reflection on earth. The enemy doesn't want you to accept this reality. But God intends that you remind yourself you have a righteousness consciousness. The consciousness of who you are in Christ helps you in several ways:

Guides Your Thinking: When your thoughts are fixated on your perfect state in Christ, obedience comes easy. Faith comes easily. Love comes easily. Do you know that part of the Bible that asks you to only think of things that are pure, just, faithful, honest? That's God asking you to maintain a righteousness consciousness. You can't be worried about how much you keep messing things up when your mind is fixed on honest thoughts. You know why? Sin consciousness holds no honesty.

Some of us are happy and joyful in other believers' presence or when in a believers' meeting. The beautiful thing is your thoughts can be pure and honest even when you're alone. Abraham was alone when the Lord called him. So was Jacob when he wrestled with God. So was Gideon when God asked him to be a Judge of Israel. If you're obsessed with your imperfections, you will restrict the flow of God's blessings your way. The devil uses negative thoughts to hinder us from beholding the beauty of God's works. But you shouldn't allow him. Put him in his place and focus on the finished work in Christ Jesus

Guides Your Conduct: The book of Proverb says, "As a man thinketh in his heart, so is he." Your thoughts directly influence your actions. Some experiences do not go simultaneously with God. For instance, you cannot finish worshipping and praising God and then start swearing at your child for not doing something you asked of him. And if by any error you do, you are quick to repent of it and receive forgiveness of sins.

Do you often do things and then instantly regret them? Do you say something grievous and then wish you could take it back? Your actions may have been influenced by your unending deliberation of the things you do not have, rather than focused on the things you have in Christ. That is exactly what righteousness consciousness does. It reminds you of the things you have in Christ, who you are in Christ, what Jesus finished on the cross for you. You can then live in wholesome peace and calmness, shining the light of God unto others

Guides Your Experiences: Righteousness opens you up to joy, to gladness, to peace of heart. You find that you are contented with the things happening in your life. No longer do you compare yourself with someone else. Instead, you are grateful for the blessings; great and small, hat you have witnessed.

Righteous thinking is not about how perfect you are or how good you measure up. Your acts of kindness do not determine it, but it fuels your acts of kindness. It speaks to how willing you are to help others grow. It speaks to how willing you are to rejoice with someone who has something you do not have.

At your workplace, a righteousness mindset would help you celebrate with a colleague who got a promotion you've been praying about too. It would help you see opportunities amidst crises. You become less judgmental, less cynical, less criticizing of yourself and others.

Know that God is pleased with you here and now. You are made in His image. You carry the seed of righteousness within you. His precious Spirit seals your salvation; you are a partaker of the covenants by faith. You have all that you need and more. You can live in this knowledge always, every single day, from now henceforth. When you choose to live by faith, every moment of your life, you live in the fullness of your identity in Christ.

LIVING BY FAITH

On January 15, 2015, a 14-year old boy fell through an ice rink while playing with his friends. He was underwater for thirty minutes before he was rescued and was rushed to the nearest Emergency Room. The boy had no heartbeat! After forty-five minutes of trying to resuscitate him, there was still no heartbeat. The room was suddenly filled with silence and grief after the doctors and nurses had fought hard to save his life. They were distraught by their failed attempts.

Just before the boy was confirmed dead, his adopted mother, Joyce Smith, arrived in total confusion. She was overwhelmed with grief and shock upon seeing her son's lifeless body. She was deeply gutted, and all she could do at that moment was offer her son to God in supplication…praying over his body. The prayer of a mother is indeed powerful! She then asked God, declared that her son be returned to her to His glory, and God heard.

That was not the end of the story. It was clearly, medically impossible that the boy would fully recover in sixteen days, but he did. For months, this story of miracle consumed the City of St. Charles County, and the boy's mother wrote a book about it and was eventually adapted into a screenplay, and then, into the 2019 feature film on Netflix, titled, 'Breakthrough.' The movie was presented in three statements as this: "Boy died; Mother prayed; Boy came back to life."

In Mark 11:23, Jesus invites us to engage our faith by saying unto a mountain, *"Go, throw yourself into the sea."* Somewhat extra, yes? We could read that scripture and think, Oh, you know, there are just other things I could do to show that I have faith. It takes faith to pray a headache away, too, yes? My faith doesn't have to be too loud, though, as long as I do the little I can do.

A lifestyle that hinges on absolute faith in God is not dismissible. This chapter is dedicated to showing you why believers can't settle for a lifestyle that's on the low side, why you need to prepare to be noticed if you will command all your affairs by faith.

The Water Walker

The water walking experience of Peter is one that broadly defines our understanding of faith in the Kingdom. The lessons we draw from this episode does not affect pastors and ministers alone but relates to everyone who identifies as a believer. This is Christianity 101 – basic lessons on living in faith. The experience begins in *Matthew 14:22-24*. *"Then Jesus made the disciples get into the boat and go-ahead to the other side of the lake, while He sent the people away. After sending the people away, He went up a hill by Himself to pray. When evening came, Jesus was there alone; and by this time, the boat was far out in the lake, tossed about by the waves because the wind was blowing against it."*

Note, it says that Jesus "made the disciples…" He strongly urged them. Why? Did Jesus know that there would be a storm waiting for them?

God doesn't give us a word that would lead us into trouble. Often, we identify with the disciples' panic and say, "C'mon, there was a storm. When you're in a storm, you easily get overwhelmed by fear."

Surely, God understands when we are afraid. He doesn't ask us not to be afraid. But God has given us His word, His precious promises. There are three hundred and sixty-five scriptures on overcoming fear, enough to go around for each day of a calendar year. We can choose to focus on the fear, the panic swept in by the storm, or we can remember the word the Lord has spoken concerning a situation. *"Between three and six o'clock in the morning Jesus came to the disciples…Then Peter spoke up, 'Lord, if it is really You, order me to come out on the water to You.' 'Come,' answered Jesus. So, Peter got out of the boat and started walking on water to Jesus." (Matthew 14:25, 28-29)*

The disciples had seen Jesus walk on water, and thinking He was a ghost, screamed out. Jesus sent His word, assuring them He was the one, and they had nothing to fear. What word has God spoken to you over a situation? I believe God has in Him a gentle nature, for once He speaks, He wouldn't come to remind you again of what He has said. It's why the Psalmist says, *"More than once I have heard God say that power belongs to Him." (Psalms 62:11)*

Obeying the invitation of Jesus to come, Peter set out to walk on water. You can have all the promises of God, but if you wouldn't act, if you do not step out based on these words, the miracle you desire to see would continue to hang midway.

"Come," Jesus says. Are you facing a hard time at work? Come. Are you in the middle of a depressing situation, and you are beginning to question if God truly cares for you? Come. Coming is a statement saying, "I believe you, God, wholly, completely. I believe what Your word says. I believe the word You spoke through my pastor, and I act by Your word. Amen!"

So, what happens when you step out in faith and the winds become boisterous? What do you do when the storms seem to overwhelm you? You keep your focus on the God who called you out and not on the storms and waves and winds. This isn't convenient for everyone to believe. But it's how faith works.

Faith says, "God has spoken this word. God made the universe. God brought back a dead boy when his mother prayed. God made provisions for an immigrant girl whose funding was cut. God provided shelter for a woman and her baby. God is bigger than these problems. Though they seem to overwhelm me now, though they seem bigger than what I can handle, my God is bigger than them, a thousand-fold and more."

We can learn from Peter's experience. The winds threatened his faith in what Jesus had spoken, but we don't have to feel threatened by the winds. We can choose to lean on Him and His word. Here's a capsule on faith in Hebrews 11:6, and it says, *"No one can please God without faith, for whoever comes to God must have faith that God exists and rewards those who seek Him."*

It is not possible to please God if you don't have faith. Yes, you are a covenanted child. Yes, you have received the promises and the blessings, but you need your faith to activate it. And look at how this faith is defined. It says, "He that cometh to God must believe that He is."

So, as you prepare to pray, as you head to church for a time of fellowship, you must believe in your heart that God is real. There are some Christians that can pray and pray and pray, and nothing happens. I have seen that. They don't believe. You must believe that He is and that He is a rewarder of them that diligently seek Him. You must connect to believe God. At no point in time should you doubt in your mind.

During a bible study session, we talked about the double portion of anointing in the church and said that a double-minded person cannot receive anything from God. A double-minded is here and there at once, but it takes a heart focused on God to receive from Him. A heart that says, "Only you, Jesus, only You."

You have in your lineage a lot of people who walked by faith. The eleventh chapter of Hebrews highlights patriarchs who demonstrated their trust in God by their faith in Him. Look at Noah. Here's a description of what transpired between God and Noah.

God says, "Noah, I need you to build an ark."

Noah says, "An ark? What's an ark?"

"It's a boat that would keep you from the flood about to happen on the earth."

"Flood? Lord, there's no rain on the earth, and yet you speak of a flood? How shall this be?"

"Oh well, you know, Noah, it's going to rain soon. It's going to rain well. I've seen the works of man, and I can't find righteousness in them. I want to preserve a generation of righteous people, and that generation would stem from you. So, you build an ark according to these dimensions."

What does Noah say? Does he argue God's reason for wanting to cause a flood? Noah goes, "Okay, Lord. Your will, Lord." The whole world was mocking him. You probably would have, too, if you had been there. It just didn't make sense. But God had said it, and it didn't have to make sense, so long it came from God.

Will you believe God if God asks you to do something that has never been done before? Will you believe God? We can easily say, "I believe in God, pastor, I have faith." However, faith is not a saying word but a doing word. Actions define faith. Your faith is evidenced by your actions.

Abraham had clocked a century in age yet still believed what God had spoken about his barrenness and his heir to come. He didn't say, "God, I am going to stop worshiping you; I am 100, Sarah is 90. There's just no way."

The Bible says even the womb of Sarah was dead. The womb was dead. It had gone from "meno-pause" to "meno-finish." What would you do if you were in a situation like Sarah? Would you think, "God, but I tried. I really did. Your promise is in my diary; it is there! Lord, I don't know how you are going to do it. I want to have faith. I really want to have faith. Just that it's hard to have faith when nothing works."

Abraham hoped against hope. His faith was a vibrant, breathing, living force. When we talk about faith, we are not talking about what you say with your mouth or the one you say when you pray. We are talking about the faith that is in your heart. That drives your actions. That is what God is looking for.

It is a faith that says, "Everything is working against me, but I believe God will do what He said He would do." Amen! Was it easy for Noah to build the ark, knowing that it had never been done before? Abraham, at the age of 100, still believed in God's promises. He was just a man like us, but he believed God with all his heart, for God is a rewarder of them that diligently seek him and ready to give all for Him. The Bible counted that as righteousness.

As a church, we need faith; as a pastor, I also need faith because there is something we don't understand; where we are today is where the level of our faith has taken us. For us to move to the next level, we must have a next-level faith. That the way spiritual things work. God will not take you to the next level if your faith is not built enough to receive it.

You can choose to be comfortable with where you are. You can choose to be a happy Christian, not causing trouble at work, having enough food to eat, having someone who loves you unconditionally. Ultimately you would realize that God intended for more than just that for you. I don't want to appear before the Father and find out I could have been more, done more, loved more, been of more help, but my faith wasn't sufficient to take me to that next level. I'm sure you do not want that either.

There are countless instructions provided on building an active faith in God. One way to do that is by praying in the Holy Ghost. Jude 20 says, *"...building up yourselves on your most sacred faith. Pray in the power of the Holy Spirit."*

The more you spend time praying in the Holy Ghost, the more your mind is tuned towards spiritual things. You become more sensitive to God's instructions. As you give yourself to prompt obedience, your faith grows. Growth in faith helps your obedience, and then obedience helps your faith. Nothing is impossible with God.

TOTAL OBEDIENCE

Faith in God is directly tied to total obedience. Again, let us look at the passage of scriptures we reviewed earlier, where God asks Abram to leave his father's house. It is recorded that *"...Abram started out...as the Lord had told him..." (Genesis 12:4, NIV)*

Do you see that? Abram went as the Lord had told him. The proof of Abram believing in what God had said to him was that he obeyed. Our obedience is the proof of our faith in God. Show me a man who has faith, who is hopeful for a miracle, who believes that nothing is impossible with God, and I will show you one who will hearken to all that God would ask them to do.

We must remind ourselves that God operates by total obedience. In mathematics, total obedience could be considered 100% obedience, and even 99.9% wouldn't cut it, for there are no abbreviations.

I would like to share a story with us that buttresses this. A group of men decided to open a business based on a conviction that God would have them do so. These men were experienced in their respective fields and had spent a good number of years climbing the corporate ladder, making pivotal calls that positively turned companies around. But they were done. It was time to go out on their own, but they needed guidance.

Of the five men, there was one who was said to be more "spiritual" than the others. Now, I should say that our metrics of determining a believer's spirituality differ significantly from God's system. We should be careful not to judge the state of a man's heart by his actions alone but also by considering the things that influence those actions.

The "spiritual" man asked that the group meet together to pray, and as they did, they obtained mercy and knew what God would want them to do concerning the intentions of their heart. They were thankful, right? They rejoiced, didn't they? Quite contrary!

Rather than rejoice, they worried over the instruction. There was little left to logic in the instruction they had received. But they had heard God right, they knew. They looked at one another and waited for the one with the biggest faith to inspire the others, but none was inspired. It simply was impossible to do exactly what God had asked them to do with the capital fund. If they went ahead, it would take years, decades even, to achieve even half of the goals they'd set for the proposed company.

So, what did they do? They acted on the instruction God spoke to them, making only a slight tweak to the details. As you would expect, the business flourished, only for a while. And then the tables turned. Over three years, the work started to shrink, and in a desperate state, they cried to God. Do you know what God said to them? He said, *"Because you did not trust in me enough to honor me…"*

Does this remind you of Moses? You know the story, don't you? We all do. Moses had led the Israelites out of Egypt, as the Lord had commanded him. As they journeyed towards the promised land, the people forgot all that God had done and instead began to complain about the good old times in Egypt. Many of us get stuck in our journey to progress because we get content with reliving the previous blessings.

We say, "I remember the good old days when everything worked out well when there was always more than enough." "Oh, I miss those times when…" God is saying, get out of the "reliving" experience. How long would you keep recounting what God has done while you miss out on what God is set to do? Gratitude teaches us to acknowledge the goodness of God, while faith teaches us to drive forward towards the better things God is working in our lives.

Moses, compelled to make provisions for the people, sought God's face, and the Lord asked him to strike the rock with a rod in his hand. On obeying, water gushed out, and the people had more than enough to drink.

Then came the second experience. *"There was no water where they camped, so the people gathered around Moses and Aaron and complained…" (Numbers 20:2-3)*

The Israelites were people who loved to recycle mistakes. You would think they would remember their earlier experience and remember that the Lord God had made provisions for them beyond their expectations. But instead, they complained about the harshness of the wilderness.

"Moses and Aaron moved away from the people and stood at the entrance of the Tent. They bowed down with their faces to the ground, and the dazzling light of the Lord's presence appeared to them."

Now, suppose you stopped reading at this point; you would be safe to think God wanted to repeat the experience of Exodus 17, where Moses struck the rock according to God's Word. But reading further, we find that God's instructions were far from a repetition.

"Take the stick that is in front of the Covenant Box, and then you and Aaron assemble the whole community. There in front of them all speak to that rock over there, and water will gush out of it. In this way, you will bring water out of the rock for the people, for them and their animals to drink." (verse 8)

I want you to imagine Moses's position. You have gone up to pray about a certain situation that is a repetition of an earlier occurrence. In prayer, God gives you an instruction that mirrors the instruction He gave you earlier. This new instruction doesn't exactly make sense to you. Didn't you apply force to the rock? Why, then, would the Lord ask you to speak?

Note the tone with which Moses spoke to the children of Israel: "Do we have to get water out of this rock for you?"

The man was worked up, and rightly so. You know, we think, "Ah, Moses should have simply obeyed the instruction to the letter. He would have entered the Promised Land if he had."

How often do we disregard a part of an instruction and hold on to the rest? Growing up, we were often told not to stay up beyond bedtime. And what did we do? We would go ahead and do exactly what we were told not to do. We didn't see it as being disobedient; we just were being "smarter."

Don't we all try to outsmart God? Outsmart an instruction? Outsmart a nudging? God says, "I want you to go right over to your neighbor's and pray for them. The husband is down with a fever, and I need you to pray for Him."

At that moment, the enemy brings up a hundred reasons why you are not qualified to pray for a sick person. "You're not a pastor, remember? Weren't you swearing at someone yesterday for disagreeing with your opinion? Surely God wouldn't hear a prayer coming from someone like you."

You find the next best alternative and obey just that. Maybe you call your pastor and ask him to come to pray for your sick neighbor. Maybe you go over and suggest that you drive them to a nearby hospital. Perhaps you assure them you are praying for them while the doctor treats them. Whatever you do, as long as it doesn't give full obedience to what God asked of you, it is not obedience.

Rather than allow the enemy to mess with your mind, say right back to him, "I have God's forgiveness. I believe that God is, and He is a rewarder of those who diligently seek Him. I'll go right on and do exactly what He asked me to do."

The next best thing is always convenient. However, our convenience isn't the priority here. God's will is the priority. God's glory is. Active faith in God works hand in hand with complete obedience. It is Jesus saying to Peter on the Sea of Galilee, "Come." It is God saying to Moses, "Speak to the rock." It is God saying to Abraham, "Get out of your father's house."

You don't need to wait for a confirmation from your pastor or your 'spiritual' friend before you obey God's prompting. You are 'spiritual' enough. You have all the 'spirituality' you need to obey God. He has made all grace available for you to do His will. He is working in you through

His Spirit to help you know and do His will. He is teaching you to demonstrate your love towards him by yielding to His will. God is calling out to you today. Would you respond?

LOVE FOR GOD AND MAN

The most recited verse in the New Testament has to be John 3:16. Simple as it appears, the verse contains mysteries that reveal the depths of God's intent towards mankind and the expression of His intent. God's love for us, displayed in the offering of His only begotten on the cross, that we all who believe might become partakers of the kingdom of His dear Son. A covenant and an invitation stronger than that which we have received through Abraham.

Love is a compelling being. As I mentioned earlier on faith, love is loud. By loud, I mean that love is always acting, hardly shrinking into the background. When a believer lives a life of love for God and man, his life becomes a witness and a testimony of the God-kind of love.

I remember when my family relocated to Canada. I had stayed back in Nigeria as I held a lucrative job at an oil company, and I still wanted to partake in the benefits of the job. I wasn't accustomed to being away from my family, but I thought I could have a few more months or years at the office. I remember my wife insisting it was time to move over, let go of the job since the family was in Canada.

From the moment she expressed her desire until I resigned, relocating was the best thing I could do. My boss was shocked by my decision. He tried to convince me otherwise. "Don't resign just yet. We can always work around something."

Love for God and Man

The only thing I needed to work around was a ticket that would take me to my wife. I am here now, and by God's grace, there is not a drop of regret. This is what love for a person can do. Love for God carries a greater weight than this. It is a living, vibrant, breathing force that holds no shame. Paul describes it as "the warm love of God" shed abroad in our hearts. This tells us that we have received the same measure of love as God, and as God loves without holding back, we have been equipped to extend a like degree of love to God and man.

This is an expression that brings us into a place of commitment, of faith, of passion. It takes a passionate heart to be fully grounded in the communication of love towards God.

As He has loved us, so are we to love Him and to love one another. God is looking for people that will demonstrate this love with passion. I believe that the church needs to get into a state of zealous love for God, love shown by our zeal to do His will, to shine His light in the world.

In Numbers 25:10, we read of a man called Phinehas. There are many lessons to learn from the account of Phinehas. "The Lord said to Moses, *"Because of what Phinehas has done, I am no longer angry with the people of Israel. He refused to tolerate the worship of any god but me, and that is why I did not destroy them in anger."*

You see how zealousness can turn away wrath because of the covenant. Verse 12 says: "So tell him I am making a covenant with him that is valid for all time to come." Not only was the wrath turned away, a new covenant of peace set up for him, a covenant of peace. "He and his descendants are permanently established as priests because he did not tolerate any rivals to Me and brought about forgiveness for the people's sin."

You see that covenant of peace was only made available for Phinehas. And every "seed after him, even the covenant of an everlasting priesthood; because he was zealous for his God and made an atonement for the children of Israel." Our service in God's vineyard is not a matter of convenience. There are blessings in God that respond to zealous service.

If you want something special before God, whatever you are given to do, whatever the Lord laid upon your heart to do, you must do it with passion. If you are praying, you pray with passion. If you are serving in the Children's Department, you should do it with passion. If you are in the choir, you better do it with passion. Do not be lukewarm in the house of God.

Acceptable service to God stems from a heart deep in love with Him. By service, I do not mean prayers alone. Our volunteering in a unit in church, the care we extend towards fellow parishioners, our offerings and our seeds, our involvement in evangelism and soul-winning, in the welfare of members, in the wellness of those who reside in our communities all these are services rendered unto God.

It is not about the man or woman who is a beneficiary of these acts of service. Truly, sometimes the response of those who receive your services dampen your joy and willingness to do more. But in those moments, you need to remember unto whom you do these things. Unto man, or God?

The passion Phinehas demonstrated for God's work opened him to a covenant of peace. Aaron, the high priest at that time, did not receive this covenant. God responds to the posture of our hearts, not the positions we have.

There was another man that God showed mercy to because of his passion. Peter, in Luke 22:31-32: *"Simon, Simon! Listen! Satan has received permission to test all of you…as a farmer separates the wheat from the chaff. But I have prayed for you, Simon, that your faith will not fail. And when you turn back to Me, you must strengthen your brothers."* This is an apostle that Satan wanted to take away. *"But I have prayed for thee, that thy faith fails not: and when thou art converted, strengthen thy brethren."*

Why did Jesus pray for Peter, but not for Judas Iscariot? Or you think that God did not know that Judas Iscariot would not betray him and collect a bribe? Jesus knew, just as He knew that Judas Iscariot was stealing the money from the poor. He knew that Judas Iscariot did not believe in the mission. And Jesus demonstrated this in several ways.

Once, Mary, the sister of Jesus, came to honor Jesus by pouring a jar of expensive oil on him. Of the twelve disciples, who took offense with that gesture? Judas! "We could have sold this fragrance for three hundred denarii and given the money to the poor," he opined.

Judas had no interest in the wellness of the poor. He advocated for the sale, knowing that the money would be put in the purse, which was left in his charge. Jesus, knowing his intentions, told him that the poor would always remain, but by Mary's gesture, she had anointed Him to prepare Him for what was to come.

Jesus knew that there was a love of money in the heart of Judas, but he would have prayed for him. But you know why he did not pray for him. Judas was a son of perdition. He had no zeal in his heart, no desire to do the will of God. His heart was not filled with passion.

Now let us consider Paul. The Bible records of Paul that he gave Jesus his boat, that He may speak to the people. As at this time, Peter was not a follower of Jesus, nor was he a disciple. Subsequently, he obeyed Jesus's instruction by casting his net on one side of the sea, raking in a large catch of fishes.

Upon the invitation to follow Jesus and be a fisher of men, there was no hesitation on Peter's end. Peter left everything and followed Jesus. This zealousness, this get-it-done attitude would continue with him as he went about with Jesus.

So, when the devil wanted to take Peter, Jesus had to ask for permission from God, and God must have said, "Look, you can take anybody but not this one." And thus, Jesus said to Peter, "When you are successful, when you are converted, you will strengthen thy brethren."

God counted on Peter's ability to command the other eleven disciples after him, given his zeal for the work. In the same manner, God had counted on Abraham to command his household after him. The heavens could not afford to lose Peter. Because if he would have lost Peter, we don't know what would have happened to the eleven.

So, you see, in everything you are doing, you need to add passion. Oh, don't serve God with a just-because mindset. Commit your whole heart to the work, knowing that God is watching you.

A few years ago, there was a sister in our church who is still with us today. She doesn't know what I am about to share with you. I saw that the devil wanted to steal her, and I remembered going to God and said, "These can go, but she is not going anywhere."

And immediately, I prayed like that; I just left it. Thank God we are still here. I told God, this one she is not going because I know what she can do, I know what she can deliver in the future for the kingdom because of the passion she has in fulfilling any assignments we give to her. When you love God, add passion to it. When the time of challenge comes, God takes record; He will trigger the covenant for you.

A few years ago, when we started the church, we didn't have money, we didn't have anything; we just started in a small place. This sister I had never met before said that God laid upon her heart to give us some evangelism items. So, she made pens with the name of the church and the address that we can use for evangelism and gave them to one of our pastors in Ottawa that gave them to me. I think it took $150 to do all these materials.

One day the person that brought the pens called me and told me, "There is a boy at the CHEO – Children's Hospital. He isn't breathing very well, and the doctors have given up on him. Pastor, can you please go with us to pray for the child?" The person who called me was also a pastor. "Why can't you go and pray for him? Why are you calling me?" I asked him.

"Pastor, you remember the pens I gave you in Gatineau? Same one, a woman, had sent for evangelism? The woman is the boy's mother," he responded to me. The Lord spoke to me immediately, saying, "Carry your Bible and go!" Brethren, stories like this one happens in real life when you have love and passion for God. I had never met this woman and her husband before, and they were not members of RCCG. I was very hesitant to go. I was mindful of being perceived as a prayer contractor. Some prayer contractors ask for money to fast for you. I don't do that. I just fast and intercede on another's behalf.

On my arrival at the hospital, I met with the doctor, who confirmed that, indeed, nothing could be done. The child's mother could not hold her tears. My heart ached as I watched her fall apart, but my expression didn't reflect my sadness (blame it on my male ego).

When I approached her, I asked, "Are you the one who sent the pens?" She said she was. I was immediately filled with faith that her son was not going to die. "Madam, your son will not die" I said to her with great conviction.

There was a Bible close to the child. I suspected they'd left it there as a mark of their faith. Some Christians believe that the Bible can work miracles. They carry the Bible everywhere, placing it under their pillows and on their worktables. The power is in the word contained in the Bible and not in the paper. If you habitually study the word of God, you would come to know the power contained in the word, not in the pages.

Love for God and Man

I asked them to fetch me water in a container. God led me to the scripture that says, "The voice of the Lord is upon the waters." I declared to the water, "May your voice enter this water, and may that water give life." Compassion rose within me, and I said, "Because this woman has shown favor to you, I decree that she finds favor with You today in Jesus Christ's name."

I instructed them to give the boy the water to drink, and I left. That child came out of the hospital two days after. What triggered it? Passion for God. The woman's passion for God's work gave her a platform for faith to operate.

God is all-knowing. He knows what lies in your future, and He alone can take care of every situation. Sometimes, He puts you in a situation that requires you to take a step of faith in service to God. Your love for God, and your passion for His work, would help you in such times.

Your love for God is also reflected in your kindness towards your fellow men. Can people see you and say you reflect God's loving nature? Do you love as Jesus did? A determination to understand and walk in God's way of love is a right step towards triggering the manifestation of God's covenants in your life.

THE ROLE OF PRAYERS

The evangelist Roberts Liardon recalls watching his grandmother, Gladoylene, show the importance of prayer in the believer's spiritual experience. In On Her Knees, a book that chronicles the life experiences of Gladoylene Moore, Roberts shares very specific details of different moments depicting his grandmother, whom he liked to call Grams, having long hours of prayers.

In one of the chronicles, Roberts writes of a time Grams was babysitting for a family and would often take an hour during the day to withdraw into a room to pray, while the baby was asleep. This was in the days when a community was connected to a single telephone line, and so whenever anyone in the community had a call, all the landlines in all the houses rang. On a particular day, Grams was at her usual hour of prayer when the phone rang.

As usual, she ignored the ringing and continued her prayers. When the ringing wouldn't stop, she headed downstairs, picked the telephone, and realizing it was in use (it was a party line and so other parties could be connected), she started to set it down.

Slightly embarrassed that her prayer could have disturbed a community, Grams decided to relocate her prayer room from the front of the house to a room at the rear of the house. She certainly wasn't going to be a disturbance. But she definitely wasn't giving up her hour of prayer. Such was her commitment to prayer and her conviction in the possibilities available to the believer who would pray.

We have access to the Father through Jesus' name. We learn to exercise our divine authority in Christ in the place of prayer. Prayer involves more than just declaring that the blessings are yours in Christ. In prayer, we can fellowship with the Father.

Hebrews 4:16 relates to us the delightful relationship we have with God. *"Let us have confidence, then, and approach God's throne, where there is grace. There we will receive mercy and find grace to help us just when we need it."* What a sweet, sweet invitation!

However, the authority that we have in the name of Jesus isn't a tool for self-aggrandizement. It's not a wand we wave to get anything we want, the way we want it. Effective prayer is one that agrees with God's word, in alignment with God's will and unity with God's purpose. It is not about what you want, but about what God would have.

This is why we do not trust our feelings in the place of prayer. I have heard many Christians say, "I just find myself struggling to pray. You know, I want to pray, but my heart is so heavy." There is grace available for you to pray. God's grace is enough and more than sufficient. You do not rely on feelings, emotions, or opinions.

Has God said it? Then you have to pray it through. The Word assures you that God will perform what He has said. John 16:24 says, *"Until now you have not asked for anything in My name; ask, and you will receive, so that your happiness may be complete."*

Do you see that? The promise is that we would have until we are full. But we can only unlock this form of fullness when we get on our knees and find what God has said concerning a situation in His word.

Many believers have given up on prayer because they are not just sure it works. Our church services reflect this. On Sundays, the auditorium is packed as worship and praises rise to God. But by midweek, when it comes time for prayer meetings, only half the church turns up. Why? It's the question we all ask. Why do people abscond prayer gatherings? Why are we eager to invite our friends to a conference, a festival, a worship service, but we keep mute when prayer programs come around? It is because we are not fully persuaded that prayer works.

I am here to tell you that prayer works. *God says, "If [my people] pray to Me and repent and turn from the evil they have been doing, then I will hear them in heaven, forgive their sins, and make their land* prosperous." *(2 Chronicles 7:14)*. That's the invitation. If you pray, God says, I will hear. But if you do not pray, if you choose to rely on your feelings or the experience someone else had in the place of prayer, then you leave me with little to do.

Some principles can guide our experience in the place of prayer. I believe that by observing these principles, you will find yourself enjoying the confidence of answered prayers.

Be Still: This isn't something common amongst believers. We get into the place of prayer with a truckload of requests, and we are barely settled before we begin to serve them up to God. Or sometimes, we just want to "groan" and "travail," and we become too loud to hear what the Lord is saying. Jesus asked that we "pray in secret…" This suggests finding a private place, but also a quiet place. Will there be a cause for you to increase your pitch in prayer? Possibly! But when you first begin to pray, be quiet. Gather your thoughts. Eliminate distractions. Stay your focus on God and not the overwhelming nature of your needs. There's no duration to how long this should be. Let your heart come into a place of quietness, and only then are you ready to proceed.

Worship: Worship speaks to the adorations we offer to God from a heart of gratitude. It's not just about the tempo of the song, how fast-paced or slow-paced it is. Worship God for who He is. Worship Him for the magnitude of His creation, for the awesome work He begun in the lives of the fathers. Let Him know how much you are in awe of Him, how thankful you are of the gift of redemption and salvation. Give due honor to the lamb. As you do this, you find that you are building momentum, that you are shifting from focusing on your needs to just wanting to enjoy the Lord's presence.

Give Thanks: In thanksgiving, you begin to speak of the things God has done in times past. Give thanks out of a heart full of joy. "In everything by prayers and supplications, with thanksgiving…" By giving thanks, you say to God, "I am constantly overwhelmed by your goodness, by the love you extend towards me, towards my family, towards my business." Your thanksgiving is a mini testimony of God's work in your life.

Make Supplications & Requests: Supplication implies that you present not just your case but even the case of others. Your love for God helps you present the needs of others in prayers. Before you pray, you should devote sufficient time to studying the Word. When you come to tender your requests, remind God of His promises in His word. God responds swiftly to His word. None of what He has said returns to Him without accomplishing that which He has sent it to do.

Believe: What is the state of your heart towards the prayers you made in God's presence? In Mark 11:22-24, Jesus teaches the disciples about the role of faith in prayers. *"…and does not doubt in his heart but believes that what he says will happen…"* Praying and entertaining doubt are conflicting actions. Your prayers should be built on faith and completed in faith.

As you stay consistent in prayers, you will find that situations begin to respond to your requests. Doubt leaves your heart, and faith fills up every fiber of your being. In prayer, you receive instructions. Some of these instructions may require that you give a substance unto God. In God's standard of measurement, prayer is as spiritual as giving. When you regard all things as spiritual unto God, your heart responds with joy and gladness.

I believe with you that God is set to do great and mighty things in your life, as you give attention to fellowshipping with God in prayers.

GENEROUS GIVING

God has a plan for our wealth/finances, and a part of that plan includes our willingness to let go of all that He has entrusted in our hands. You know, the subject of giving has become a sensitive one to address in the church nowadays. It is no longer strange to overhear believers arguing about what a particular church is doing with their offerings and tithes.

Dear believer, please allow me to encourage you with the truth as contained in the Bible. You should look to cultivating a lifestyle of giving because all who give position themselves for an increase. Operating in all the covenants of God requires a form of sacrificial parting. From Abraham and the covenants God made with Him to make of Him a great nation, down to the new covenant God establishes with us on this day, something is given.

Our salvation experience is built on the giving of the only begotten son. When God blessed Abraham with a son, as he had said, he asked Abraham to give the boy as a sacrifice unto Him. This, God did, to both educate and prove Abraham's heart, whether he would love Isaac (the gift) more than the Lord God (the giver).

The Bible says in Luke 6:38, *"Give to others, and God will give to you. Indeed, you will receive a full measure, a generous helping, poured into your hands – all that you can hold. The measure you use for others is the one that God will use for you."*

It is not the amount of money you give that is important to God, but the proportion of your gift relative to all that God has blessed you with.

This is a mindset we should be open to adopting, that when we cheerfully give, we are not doing it towards a validation from God; it is not so that we can get in return (though God would have us be blessed as we give). Giving, the kind that is both cheerful and generous comes from knowing that the earth is the Lord's, and He is the One who gives everything we have now.

God is not interested in whether you give $1,000 or $100 or $1. But you know what God is interested in? God is interested in the proportion you give. The question that God will ask you is this, "Are you giving sacrificially, or you are giving because it is convenient for you? Are you a cheerful giver? Are you a generous giver or a convenience giver?"

Let us consider the widow of Zarephath. There was a famine in the land; she had only one meal left. But God told Elijah, "Go; I have prepared a widow for you to take care of you." Why did God not send Elijah to an affluent person? Why is it that God did not send Elijah to the palace? Why is it that God did not send Elijah to a person who had abundance? He sent Elijah to a widow.

I have said it several times, if God wants to bless you, he will send you to somebody with a need, and He wants to see how you will react to that person. God will not bless a man whose hands are tight. Because when your hand is tight, even to receive is difficult.

The widow would have calculated; in fact, she calculated. The man of God said, "Give me water." She brought the water without grumbling. Water wasn't as scarce as food.

The Blood Covenant

Then the man of God asked her to bring a morsel of bread, and she told him she had only a handful of flour left, with which she'd intended to make a meal for herself and her son, which they would eat, and then die.

What did the man of God say? He said, "Make me a small portion from the meal first." What a test of faith! God could have sent this man to a family that had plenty with enough to share. Instead, He chose the widow for an opportunity to be blessed. Every opportunity you have to help, give, don't miss it, don't miss it. The Bible says that the widow cooked for the man of God, and she had plenty throughout the famine season.

Recently, two youths in our church were of help to one of the students that just arrived. When I heard what they did, I said those are the kind of people I want around me. They did not know her before; they were just ready to make everything they can to make her comfortable. They triggered the covenant.

We had a situation in the church before; it is why we have a bathroom in the church's basement. There was a man who came here once and told me his story, and I said, "Very good, we will get you a place where you can stay." Nobody wanted to take him, not even the brethren in the church. We tried to rent a room for him, which also proved difficult since he has not a guarantor of any kind, so I reasoned that if we had a bathroom in the church's basement, it is possible to accommodate such a person at least temporarily. Thank God we were eventually able to make this happen.

Generous Giving

The fourth chapter of 2 Kings tells the story of another woman who also extended generosity towards Elisha. She noticed that Elisha was always passing her gate to go to another city. She invited him into her house and served him lunch. The bible says that the first time the man of God came and ate, it was very delicious, so he kept going. The bible says that every time Elisha stopped by, he would go in, sit down and eat, even if he was not invited in. His ministry received a redirection because of the woman's invitation.

Then the woman said to the man of God that she had prepared a room where he can rest. And the man of God accepted. But she did not know that there was a problem ahead and that the only man that can solve it was this man of God. Elisha started sleeping in the upper room. The man started sleeping upstairs. Such was the immense nature of the woman's generosity that the man of God told his servant to ask the woman what she wanted from him.

Do you see how powerful that is? She did all of it without asking anything. She wasn't looking for recognition; she wasn't hoping for a need. She said to the man of God, "I have all I need here among my people."

Can you do the same thing? Without seeking for somebody to say thank you. We should appreciate people who give to us, but when we give, how easily can we give without expecting to receive in return?

The servant of the man of God had to dig to know that this woman did not have a child. Upon learning that she was without a child, Elisha called her and told her that she would have a child this time next year. The woman laughed. She must have thought the man of God was joking, for she said, "Please, sir, don't lie to me. You are a Man of God!"

I imagine that she must have gotten past the age of childbearing. Like Sarah, who had given up all hopes of a child, this woman had removed the possibilities of being a mother from her list of expectations.

We see that this woman got a child the year after God's word came to her through the man of God. Her life remains an example of generous giving, without any attachment.

Allow me to teach you something that I practice myself. Don't wait until you have plenty before you imbibe a heart of generous giving. You know, when pastors come to the church and preach, I always give them an honorarium. I give them. It is not about the money we give them; it is about the blessing that comes with giving. That is why this church will never lack. Everything we want to do, God has always been faithful.

But you see, that is the way we have been brought up as children of God. We honor our pastor; we honor their family, and we give to them as a church. The exceptions, which are often few, are in cases when the man of God says, "Don't worry, it is okay. I am not going to take it." That is different. But if that man of God accepts it, we will give it. Amen. Some people say that it is as if we pay for the ministration, that we are paying for the service.

Can you buy life? Any man of God that ministers unto you releases an element of life. This life is not one that can be measured by silver or gold. It is eternal; it cannot be bought with money. The woman who fed

Elisha recognized what blessings the man of God could speak over her. She triggered a covenant of blessing by honoring the man of God.

Make giving the center of your life.

I come from an impoverished background. I mean severe poverty. I was praying, Lord, "Deliver me from poverty, deliver me from poverty." My wife was still gracious to marry me, even in my poverty, and I appreciate it today. But one day, the Lord spoke to my heart. He instructed me to give 500 Naira to a brother and give all the clothes I have to the needy. As I was praying, someone knocked at my door, and this brother came in.

The mercy of God had led him to him. I was surprised by how early he'd come looking for me. Perhaps I would have understood if I was a pastor. But back then, I was only a brother. "Please, I need 500 Naira to start a business," he said. I asked him to sit down, and I went from room to room until I found a place to borrow the money. Returning, I gave it to him, and I asked him to go start his business. I didn't need to wait for a loud voice from heaven to know it was what God would have me do.

I took all my clothes and gave them to the church's welfare team. I remember that the following Sunday, I could spot several people dressed in those outfits. I didn't understand it then, but I knew it was what God would have me do.

But brethren, my destiny was changed within three months. That was when I understood the power of giving because I had done all kinds of prayer. I have always been a prayer warrior, but nothing seemed to be working until that generosity triggered the covenant, and I am here today in front of you.

The Blood Covenant

I want to share with you a principle on giving that I have learned in my faith walk. When God asks you to give, He isn't removing you from your resources. Instead, He is redirecting your resources. Suppose you're at home with your family, watching a ministration on television, and then you feel led to give a seed offering of one hundred dollars ($100) towards the ministry. Perhaps it's not the church you attend, but you are certain God wants you to give. When you take the $100 out of $1000, logically, you are left with $900. But under God, you have $900 and $100 in transit.

Now, here's the sweet part! That $100 has within it the potential to return to you as $500, as $1000, or even as $10,000. There's no mathematics to how the return comes. As long as you give from a heart of generosity and your faith is active, you will receive the return.

Often, we expect God to bless us in the same way we gave. But God is full of wisdom. His thoughts are not our thoughts. You expect God to prick the heart of someone to send you $500 for the $100 you gave. What God does is to prompt someone to send you the link to a job opening with a monthly payment that triples what you're currently earning. Or God reaches out to your mother and heals her persistent pneumonia.

I encourage you to focus on what you are giving to God and not what you seek to get from Him. Should you expect a harvest? Certainly. But can you determine in what way the harvest would come to you? Certainly not!

Generous Giving

I am forever thankful for my wonderful wife, who agreed with me in faith back when she could have questioned my obedience to God's instructions. She continues to believe together with me, and I am learning that obeying God pays always.

God will always allow you to choose what you would do. Would you step out in faith, and cast your bread upon the waters, cast your seed into God's hands? Or would you hold on tightly to what God has given to you? God would have you be a generous giver. But the choice is yours.

BALANCING YOUR FAITH WITH WORKS

Earlier, we looked at how giving unlocks certain possibilities made available to us in God's covenants of blessings and increase. We also discussed the activeness of faith extensively and how vital it is for believers to be rock solid in the faith.

A man attended a church service where the pastor preached on faith and hope. The sermon was inspiring, the right words the man needed to hear. After the service, he stayed back on one of the pews; his head bowed as if in prayer.

A few hours later, the last set of church workers prepared to leave when someone spotted the man. She approached him and asked if everything was okay.

"Yes," the man said. "Just waiting," he concluded. At that moment, his phone rang. He glanced at the caller once and frowned. Upon noticing the worker's curious look, he explained that the caller was his boss. He had something to deliver before dusk, but he had to wait.

"How about heading home to finish the work and then coming back to see the pastor?"

The man smiled. He wasn't waiting to see the pastor. He was waiting on God, as the pastor had preached that the mark of a believer's faith was his willingness to wait on God until the answer came.

Like this man, many of us have gone about the whole business of faith and works the wrong way. On one end, we feel that faith in God is complete in itself, and so doesn't need to be backed by works. If God has said that He would do it, then He would, and there's little or nothing I need to do other than wait for Him to do what He has said to do.

On the other end, we feel that faith must always be boosted by the things we do. If we choose to stay idle and not work, then nothing may happen, and we may spend an entire lifetime searching for an inexistent miracle.

There's a call for us to redefine what we understand by "works." Have you ever ridden a bicycle? Understanding faith and works can be likened to pedaling a bike. When you set off pedaling, you move both pedals in the same direction. You can also compare it to walking. I don't suppose it's possible to walk on one leg all day while the other leg lies idle.

Our "works" are the actions we take in tandem with our faith. Your prompt obedience to get on your knees and pray down a miracle for a family that attends your church is your "works." The three hours you commit to studying for the exam you just prayed about are the "works" in that given situation.

Your works are your actions, thoughts, expectations, and expressions that align with what you believe God for and what you have faith for. Know that your works do not stand in the way of your faith in God. Rather, they back up your faith in God.

You don't pray for wisdom in a particular situation and then go thinking, "What if I say something stupid? What if I make a wrong judgment call?" Just as you wouldn't move your left leg forward and your right leg backward, your works and your faith cannot contradict. They complement one another. Let us examine the experiences of Abraham again in Genesis 12: *"The LORD said to Abram, 'Leave your country, your relatives, and your father's home, and go to a land that I am going to show you. I will give you many descendants, and they will become a great nation. I will bless you and make your name famous so that you will be a blessing. I will bless those who bless you, But I will curse those who curse you. And through you, I will bless all the nations."* (verses 1-3)

The Bible does not come out to tell us that Abraham trembled at the word of God and believed God. Yet, we have a record that Abraham believed. How? "...Abram...started from Haran as the Lord had told him to do..." (Genesis 12:4)

We find here Abram's swift obedience to God's instructions. This perhaps is the most excellent demonstration of faith – that upon receiving the word of God, you swiftly obey, doing all that is required of you. That is how you back up your faith with works.

It is time for you to get to work. You have within you all that you need to partake of the covenants of faith. Do not be like the woman who, traveling by train for the first time, waited at the train station with her ticket in her hand. When the train pulled in, she watched passengers climb on board. She noticed none of the passengers were bringing out their tickets, and so she wondered in her heart if she was at the wrong station.

As the train pulled away, a stranger approached her and asked why she didn't get on the train.

"Oh! That's...that is not my train," she said.

"But you have the ticket," he said, nodding at the thin slip in the grasp of her palm.

"Oh! I didn't see them use it."

He smiled, "They only tender it once the train starts moving. Everyone knows not to get on board without a ticket, so the conductor doesn't take the ticket when folks board." Then turning away, he muttered, "You should have asked someone."

You have the tickets to access the blessings in Christ Jesus. You have the gift of salvation, confirmed by the witnessing of the Holy Spirit within you. You have the word of God that is filled with the promises of God for your life and what God has said about you. You have in your lineage men and women who, through faith, did great exploits. You have the wisdom of God. You have a high priest that lives to make intercessions for you. You have the blood of Jesus Christ, the blood that speaks better things than the blood of Abel. You have the fellowship of the brethren. You have resources, such as this book, that equips you with the knowledge of your place in Christ.

You do not have the spirit of fear. You are not condemned. You are not forsaken. You are not helpless, not abandoned, not weak. You are not given to worry or fear.

I challenge you today to walk in the realities of all that is yours in Christ. Let the word of God shape your confessions, your beliefs, your thoughts, the desires of your heart. Replace negative thoughts with positive confessions. Be deliberate about renewing your mind by the word. Associate yourself with like-minded people, people who sharpen your faith. The Bible speaks about "iron sharpening iron," and so you must remain in the company of people whose words, whose conducts, sharpen your beliefs and expectations.

Cultivate and sustain an intimate fellowship with God through Christ. Give attention to prayer. Through prayers, you would come to know much more than you presently do. God is for you. He is with you. He is in you. He is making a way for you in the wilderness and rivers in the desert. Do you see it? Yes, yes, see it. Visualize it. Live in it.

I desire to help you understand the blessings of God for your life. Every day can be a blessed experience in God. This is His will for your life. You have the power to choose to walk in it. I believe you will make that choice today.

EPILOGUE

When we come into Christ, we are filled with a desire to partake of all the perks and benefits of salvation. We also want to live in the grandest houses and drive the coolest cars and work the most rewarding jobs. We want to raise kids who don't disobey the law or disregard traffic lights, or party all night. We want neighbors who say, "Bless you" when crossed and sing "Glory, Hallelujah" on Saturday evenings. We want partners who are loving and faithful. We want to spend the summer holidays with our grandkids, to have enough money to give to missionaries and orphanages and charity causes.

You find that the average Christian's life becomes a pursuit after the same things that he has received in Christ. How much work must I do to have the most admirable job in town? If only I could pray and fast more, then maybe God would send someone to give me money for groceries. I think God is angry with me because I said something stupid about my colleague at work, and that's why God is rebuking me with this sickness.

No! Not God! The Bible shows us God's wish is that *"…everything may go well with you and that you may be in good health – as I know, you are well in spirit."* (Jude 2)

This book is all about showing you how to access the blessings of covenants by faith. Let us return to the beginning. Salvation comes by believing. The blood of Jesus cleanses your sins and purifies you. God's love for you earns you the free gift of salvation. If you want to grow, start by giving attention to praying and the study of the word. Remember, your experiences mirror what the Bible says about you.

There is an interconnectedness to all these. Being prosperous does not exclude you from enjoying the blessings of multiplication. As you engage faith to receive, you must not neglect the power of prayers, or the possibilities through cheerful giving, or the culture of work.

Do not isolate any one of these principles. The Bible records that Abraham "…received what God had promised." You are in Abraham, and by faith, you have received the blessings of these promises, these covenants. There's so much for you to experience in Christ.

So, take the steps. Connect to the covenants. Pray without ceasing. Be committed to God's work. Cast seeds with joy. Commit towards prosperity, good health, and increase. Know what you have received in Christ and begin today to walk in them. If you have come to know Jesus through this book and are eager to continue in this blood covenant, then you should join a fellowship near you where God's word is preached.

For prayers or counseling, you can also send me an email at olusegun.raji@gmail.com. May God bless you always.

ABOUT THE AUTHOR

Pastor Olusegun Raji is the head pastor of Chapelle De La Résurrection and the zonal pastor for QC1 of the Redeemed Christian Church of God. He oversees all the departments of the church and often preaches on Sundays. He is also an experienced professional, with more than 28 years of experience in and outside Canada, specializing in Business Analysis, System Administration, Project Management, and Supply Chain Management with over 18 years' experience with fortune 500 companies developing and implementing improvement programs and processes for the good of the company.

www.ingramcontent.com/pod-product-compliance
Lightning Source LLC
Chambersburg PA
CBHW072038110526
44592CB00012B/1472